THE
IRAN
AGENDA

THE
IRAN
AGENDA

The Real Story of U.S. Policy and the Middle East Crisis

REESE ERLICH

Foreword by Robert Scheer

PoliPointPress

The Iran Agenda: The Real Story of U.S. Policy and the Middle East Crisis

This edition published in the United States of America by PoliPointPress, P.O. Box 3008, Sausalito, CA 94966-3008
www.p3books.com

Production management: BookMatters
Book design: BookMatters
Cover design: Jeff Kenyon
Cover photography © Henri Bureau/Sygma/Corbis

Library of Congress Cataloging-in-Publication Data

Erlich, Reese W., 1947–
    The Iran agenda : the real story of U.S. policy and the Middle East crisis / by Reese Erlich ; foreword by Robert Scheer.
        p.   cm.
    Includes bibliographical references and index.
    ISBN-13: 978-0-9778253-5-6 (alk. paper)
    ISBN-10: 0-9778253-5-3 (alk. paper)
        1. United States—Foreign relations—Iran. 2. Iran—Foreign relations—United States. 3. Arab-Israeli conflict—1993–
4. Middle East—Politics and government—1945–
I. Title.
    E183.8.I55E75   2007
    327.73055—dc22   2007026899

Printed in the United States of America
July 2007

Published by:
PoliPointPress, LLC
P.O. Box 3008
Sausalito, CA 94966-3008
(415) 339-4100
www.p3books.com
Distributed by Ingram Publisher Services

This book is dedicated to the people
of Iran and the United States,
both of whom want peace.

Contents

Foreword

Robert Scheer

Historical mischief has stark consequences, not at all mitigated when world leaders, including Americans, claim the best of intentions. Steeped in the mythology of innocence since our own revolt against British imperial rule, the United States has consistently presented its own imperial drive as an effort to extend rather than suppress the freedoms of the peoples conquered.

The pattern has repeated itself many times since the Second World War, but it has never been clearer than in the persistent but disastrous effort of the United States to direct the politics of oil-rich Iran. Never admitting to an overriding interest in controlling that nation's and the region's precious resource, U.S. leaders have always insisted that they care only to expand the universe of peace and freedom. That charade now stands exposed since the U.S. invasion of Iraq. But despite that debacle, the longer-standing goal of dominating Iran remains all the more compelling to the United States.

In this perceptive analysis, Reese Erlich writes in the spirit of Graham Greene, whose classic *The Quiet American* captured the naive but nonetheless murderous impact of U.S. intervention in the "third world" of the Cold War era. Like Greene, Erlich blends an on-the-scene familiarity with everyday life in the target country with a piercing critique of the purportedly high motives of the foreign invader.

The United States has interfered with Iran for more than fifty years, and the consequences of that sorry history will continue to haunt us well into the future. Our capricious disregard for the nationalist and religious complexity of Iran began with the 1953 overthrow of its last democratically selected leader, the secular populist Mohammad Mossadegh. His crime was to begin the nationalization of foreign oil companies. He assaulted our sacred faith in the divine right of corporate plunder that trumped all other concerns, including the will of the Iranian people to control their own resources, and hence their own destiny.

After a well-documented coup paid for and engineered by the CIA, the United States replaced Mossadegh with the self-proclaimed Shah of Shahs, Mohammad Reza Pahlavi, who based his legitimacy on a highly questionable royal lineage. Despite U.S. and Israeli support, the shah's regime eventually collapsed under the weight of its own corruption and selfish opulence, which wasted oil revenues on an array of unnecessary purchases, including U.S. military hardware. The shah was replaced by religious fanatics who claimed the mantle of incorruptibility. Because the shah had governed in the name of modernization, it is no wonder that the ayatollahs' appeal to the glories of a fundamentalist world found a following among those whom the shah had ignored.

It is also no wonder that the theocrats who ascended to power should prove hostile to Israel and the United States. But of course, given the general acceptance of American virtue in foreign policy, the 1979 taking of hostages by the Iranian revolutionaries was interpreted as a totally unprovoked attack. American politicians and media figures have accepted this interpretation uncritically. Although the Iranian leadership has undergone many changes since then—from militant to somewhat reasonable and back again—most Americans have never wavered from the view that Iranian leaders are nothing but treacherous.

Call it the cartooning of Iran, in which the motives and actions of Iran's various (and sometimes competing) leaders are never plumbed for profound explanations but rather dismissed as the pure caprice of the malevolent. Hence, we see the all-too-easy classification of Iran as part of the "axis of evil" by the incoming Bush Administration. That designation is now an embarrassment, given that Bush's invasion of Iraq has left the Iraqi disciples of the Iranian ayatollahs very much in power in Baghdad.

Erlich provides an invaluable insight into the contradictions that drive U.S. policy toward Iran and threaten to take us into yet another disastrous war in a region that has ample reason to question U.S. motives. He questions the demonization of Iran's leadership without underestimating the theocracy's record of suppressing the people it rules. Having witnessed modern ideological wars, he brings a nuanced and—dare one say it?—objective view of the contending forces attempting to define modern Iran. The book is particularly useful in dissecting the trite, politically motivated threat assessments of Iran's nuclear program and its alleged support of international terrorism. In both instances, there are painful reminders of the phony case made to justify the invasion of Iraq.

Erlich's analysis opens up possibilities for change other than those that rely on the military option, which has proved so disastrous in neighboring Iraq. Indeed, Erlich questions the value of a belligerent U.S. stance when its primary impact is to enhance the popularity of hardliners and undermine those working for genuine reform in Iran. For that reason, this is a hopeful book, as well as a well-written work on a difficult subject, for it suggests the truly revolutionary prospect that the Iranian people might be trusted with the difficult task of engineering their future. After a half century of heavy-handed U.S. interference, they can hardly do a worse job on their own.

But Iran is not some banana republic to be toyed with as a matter of whim; it is rather the historic seat of a major civilization whose legacy, both politically and religiously expansionist, cannot be ignored. A U.S. foreign policy based on ignorance of Iran's rich history and preoccupied only with U.S. interests has wrought horrible consequences. Those consequences— unintended as they sometimes were, and authored by politicians oblivious to the complexity of the world upon which they intruded—now dominate the key drama of international politics. The value of this excellent treatise is that it exhibits rare humility in attempting to grasp why modern-day Iranians have proved so difficult for the U.S. government to deal with. While critical of the clerical tyranny that has controlled Iranian politics since the anti-shah revolution, Erlich avoids the path of crude demonization that has characterized most popular writing on this subject. Instead, he skillfully melds personal observations with a scholar's insight into the historical record that informs today's passions—passions that we ignore at our peril.

ONE

In Tehran with Sean Penn

All our senses were assaulted simultaneously as we walked slowly down the inclined road into the Tehran bazaar. We smelled the fragrance of savory kebabs, heard the cacophony of merchants hawking their wares, and saw the yellow saffron rice and deep purple eggplant. It was June 2005.

The crowds jostled Sean Penn, Norman Solomon, and me as we worked our way deep into the narrow byways of the bazaar. Sean was there on assignment for the *San Francisco Chronicle*; Norman was writing for his media analysis column; and I was reporting as a freelancer for the *Dallas Morning News* and Canadian Broadcasting Corporation Radio. I had visited the bazaar during my previous trip in 2000 and figured this was a good way for Sean and Norman to get acquainted with ordinary people.

Middle East bazaars were the first shopping malls. Tehran's main bazaar consists of a vast underground network of stalls, shops, and stores. You can buy anything from ridiculously expensive hand-knotted Persian silk carpets to ladies' underwear. Both are clearly displayed for passersby. There are no fixed prices. Bargaining is a proud tradition in Iran. If you pay the first price asked, you are clearly not from around these parts.

As we walked past the many shoppers, our translator and guide, Maryam Majd, suddenly became aware that this would be no ordinary visit to the bazaar. "Everyone is whispering Sean's name," she said a bit apprehensively. Although I don't speak Farsi, I could hear the mumbled recitation "Sean Penn" and see the startled looks on people's faces. We had arrived in Tehran two days before, without any prior announcement. So most people were very surprised to see the world-famous actor, with his wavy hair and piercing eyes, just ambling by.

In meetings at Sean's house north of San Francisco before our departure, we all agreed that the purpose of the trip was to learn the views of Iranians toward the United States and their own government. Sean was visiting as a writer, not an actor or celebrity. He did not want to become the focus of the story and refused to give any media interviews.

"Do you think they know me over there?" he asked me during one preparation session. "Oh yes," I responded. But none of us had any idea *how* well known Sean was in Tehran—nor the buzz his trip would have, even years later.

We were walking in the bazaar, looking at the incredible array of clothing, household goods, food, and antiques. We stopped at a stall where Moshtabor was selling small home appliances such as irons and blenders. He asked that we use only his first name.[1] We asked him about the U.S. assertion that Iran's quest for nuclear power disguises a plan to build nuclear weapons. Moshtabor said Iran is not building nuclear weapons. He defended Iran's desire to have nuclear power.

"Every country needs to have access, and it's our right," he told us.

Moshtabor told us that compared to the 1980s, cultural restrictions are much more relaxed in Iran. The government usually looks the other way if people choose to drink alcohol in their own homes or see their girlfriends without male relatives present. The government won't allow most western films to be shown in theaters or on television, but the films are readily available on pirated DVDs. In fact, major Hollywood films often reach Tehran before being released in the United States. Moshtabor told us that many Iranian young people are obsessed with Hollywood movie stars.

At that point Sean, who had been interviewing someone else, walked over to join us. "That guy looks just like Sean Penn," Moshtabor told us with a big grin. Suddenly he realized that he was talking to the real Sean Penn. "I'm going to see *The Interpreter*," he blurted out. "I know you were married to Madonna."

Great. We've come halfway round the globe to meet ordinary Iranians and discuss matters of grave international concern. And Iranians want to talk to us about Madonna.

That encapsulates the contradictions in today's Iran. Ten thousand people chant "Death to America" at Friday prayers. But afterwards, those same people invite us home for lunch. In part, that reflects traditional Iranian hospitality toward strangers. But it's also a genuine friendliness and fascination with things American. Many Iranians studied in the United States in the 1960s and 1970s. I've met Iranians who speak with a Bostonian or even a valley girl accent.

But many Iranians strongly criticized U.S. government policy. Yes, they are bombarded with clerical propaganda de-

nouncing the United States and Israel. But they also haven't
forgotten the U.S. support for the shah's dictatorship[2] or the
American navy ship that shot down an Iranian civilian airliner, killing all 290 people on board.[3] They may love Sean
Penn, but they would take up arms against George Bush.

Why We Hate *Them*

Since the 1979 revolution overthrew the U.S.-backed shah,
successive Democratic and Republican administrations have
vilified Iran. They have argued that Iran poses a threat to U.S.
national security, with the reason varying by the year: It
spreads Islamic revolution; it supports terrorists; it plans to
develop a nuclear bomb; it kills American soldiers in Iraq.
That hostility has remained, even when some of the U.S. jus-
tifications have disappeared. For example, the United States
rarely mentions Iran's trying to spread its Islamic revolution
anymore, because Iran largely stopped doing so in the 1980s.
The United States just shifts the goalposts and comes up with
new ways to score the game.

U.S. policy is controlled by a relatively small ruling elite of
corporate executives, military leaders, government bureaucrats, and politicians. That elite is supposed to be subject to
democratic control. In practice, however, the American people
have little influence over its decisions.

The U.S. ruling elite always wants to confuse national se-
curity with corporate/military interests. The people of the
United States face no immediate threat from Iran. Iran cannot
and would not launch a military attack on U.S. territory.
While it supports groups that have used terrorist tactics in
Israel and other parts of the Middle East, it is no supporter of

Al Qaeda or other terrorist organizations that pose a real threat to the United States.[4] If the current government of Iran disappeared tomorrow, Americans would be no more or less secure.

But Iran does threaten the interests of the political, military, and corporate elite who run the United States.

The Great Game in the Internet Era

In the early part of the nineteenth century, Britain competed with Russia, the Ottoman Turks, and other imperialist powers to control the oil wealth of the Middle East. Oil was vital to power navy ships and home-front industry. The British had no oil of their own, so they had to control colonies and neo-colonies that did. The imperialist powers called this scramble for natural resources the Great Game. For them it was a game; for the people of the region, it was deadly.

Today the players have changed, but the Great Game continues. Charles Freeman, Jr., was U.S. Ambassador to Saudi Arabia (1989–92) and Under Secretary of Defense for International Security Affairs (1993–94). He welcomed me into his office at the Middle East Policy Council in Washington DC. He was jovial and outspoken as he explained U.S. national interests in Iran.

"There is a hierarchy of American interests at stake, which begin with secure access to energy supplies," he told me.[5] U.S. oil companies never come pounding on his door demanding that the United States overthrow the Iranian regime or invade Iraq, he explained. They don't have to. U.S. politicians and military men understand that the country must have secure sources of oil. And the oil companies automatically benefit.

Freeman said the United States wants Middle Eastern governments "that are not hostile, countries that are willing to work with American companies to provide energy. It means governments that are sufficiently competent to maintain stability rather than engage in acts that disrupt the flow of energy."

Iran sits on approximately 10 percent of the world's proven oil supplies and has the second-largest amount of natural gas.[6] Iran also sits between the Persian Gulf and the Caspian Sea, two critical oil regions. The world's oil tankers slip down Iran's coast at the Strait of Hormuz, which narrows to thirty-one miles at one point. Control of that strait means control of the whole region. No wonder the British, Russians, Germans, and Americans have all sought to dominate Iran.

Freeman also noted that because the United States buys so much oil from the region, it needs to sell products to keep a favorable balance of trade. "This is a significant market for our products and services. We have to sell things to the people who sell oil in order to buy oil. Dollars that we give them have to be recycled."

Freeman said U.S. generals and admirals worry about the Strait of Hormuz as well. "The United States is a global power. We have forces both in Europe and Asia. From a military point of view, this is a vital choke point. It's vital that it stay open."

Paul Pillar was the CIA's national intelligence officer for the Near East and South Asia (2000–05). He is now professor at Georgetown University's Security Studies Program. He told me, "Everyone is quite conscious, not least of all U.S. military planners, about the capability of the Iranians to cause—if they had the motive to do so—a lot of mischief in regard to

closing the strait or necessitating considerable military meas-
ures on the opposite side to keep it open, that is to say, on the
part of the United States."[7]

The U.S. ruling elite not only wants to dominate the region
but works to prevent any other country from doing so. Since
its inception in 1979, the clerical government in Iran has
wagged its collective turban at U.S. oil companies and military
brass. Robert Hunter, U.S. ambassador to NATO from 1993 to
1998, said the U.S. "goal with Iran is not even regime change,
but regime change as a means to eliminating Iran as a com-
petitor for power and influence."[8]

Please note, dear reader, than none of these "national interests" have much to do with you and me. Sure, we need petroleum to drive cars and natural gas to power electricity
plants. But the United States can buy those energy resources
on international markets, as do other countries. In order to
maintain a steady supply of oil, Sweden doesn't unilaterally
impose sanctions, prop up dictatorships, or overthrow governments. Apparently, God has given that mandate to the
United States of America. In reality, U.S. strategic interests
benefit corporations whose profits depend on domination of
the region.

Aha! some neoconservatives are mumbling to themselves
right now. If you oppose U.S. policy, you must be a supporter
of the Iranian mullahs. Actually, no. Iran is ruled by a reactionary, dictatorial clique that oppresses its own people. However, that doesn't make Iran a threat to Americans. As we will
see in later chapters, those Iranians fighting hardest to get rid
of Iran's government are also strong opponents of U.S. policy.

The U.S. ruling elite can't very well tell the American people that we may go to war with Iran to improve the long-term

profits for Exxon Mobil and Halliburton. So the United States creates threats, or exaggerates those that do exist.[9] And that's one of the reasons we visited Iran.

Visiting the Ghost of Khomeini

Sean, Norman, and I visited one of the most highly guarded locations in Tehran, a place where ordinary Iranians never go. It's the compound where Ayatollah Ruhollah Khomeini once ruled, and today it is home to some of the country's top officials.

In the early years of the revolution, Ayatollah Khomeini spoke to throngs of followers while seated on the second-story balcony of his home. That's where we visited. They've preserved Khomeini's living quarters since his death, as a kind of museum that Iranians can't visit.

"This is the famous balcony," said Mohammed Hashemi, a grizzled old man and former Khomeini bodyguard. "This is where he first called the USA the Great Satan. This is where everything started. This is the place," he said with a hearty chuckle.[10]

We were there to interview Hassan Khomeini, grandson of the late ayatollah, who now heads the influential Khomeini Foundation. Hassan Khomeini welcomed us into a meeting room in his grandfather's house. He sported a ginger-colored beard, wore long white clerical robes, and wrapped his head in the black turban indicating he was a descendant of the prophet Mohammed. Some of us sat on chairs. Others rested, Iranian style, on thick carpets and cushions.

We asked for his response to U.S. charges that Iran is a major sponsor of terrorism. "What is the yardstick that defines Iran as a terrorist-supporting nation yet dismisses such a claim against Israel?" he said.[11]

Bush uses the issue as an excuse, he said. If Iran met all U.S. demands, Bush would come up with new ones. "I don't know about his intentions" about a military attack, he told us. "It will be clear in the future. I don't believe the USA has enough power to attack Iran. American public opinion, as well as what America is facing in Iraq, as well as world situation, won't allow the Americans to do that."

Khomeini conceded that U.S.-Iran relations have been bad for a long time, but he blamed President George W. Bush for making things worse. After all, it was Bush who referred to Iran as part of the "axis of evil."

"The first thing is to recognize the Iranian government as an independent government," Khomeini told us. "The U.S. public should force its government to change its opinion in this regard."

A Wrestler, the Foreign Ministry, and a Cup of Coffee

Two days later we covered a women's rights demonstration in front of the University of Tehran. Plainclothes police and fundamentalist paramilitaries known as Basijis blocked hundreds of people from attending the demonstration and strong-armed the press. Sean got shoved around by a cop. Dozens of Iranians were clubbed by the police. The government even turned off cell phone service in that part of Tehran to block communication among demonstrators.

We got back to the hotel that night tired and angry. By this time, Sean's visit was making headlines all over Iran. So the hotel assigned a three-hundred-pound former wrestler to es-

cort Sean while inside the hotel and shoo people away while
we were in the lobby. The wrestler had secured a table for
Hamid-Reza Asefi, then Iran's deputy foreign minister, who
had decided to stop by for an unannounced chat with us.

Boy, did he pick the wrong night.

I pulled out my microphone, hooked up the cables to the
recorder, and let fly. Why did the police attack peaceful
demonstrators demanding equal rights for women? I asked.
"If [the demonstrators] had permission, they should be protected," he answered rather lamely.[12] He knew that it's impossible to get official permission for demonstrations critical
of the government. So demonstrators are always subject to
attack and arrest.

Sean followed up by asking Asefi if it's government policy
for police to beat up reporters. Asefi claimed that the government works transparently with journalists. "I don't know
why they [beat people]. They were wrong." In fairness to
Asefi, he was part of reformist President Mohammad
Khatami's government. A parallel intelligence service within
the judiciary, Revolutionary Guard, and Basijis operated independently of any governmental control and sometimes
even jailed Khatami supporters.

But neither was Asefi willing to criticize those forces
within the government who trampled on people's basic rights.
He reminded us that Iran was far more democratic than Saudi
Arabia or other Middle East dictatorships supported by the
United States. True, but also irrelevant. Iran says it is an
Islamic democracy but hardly lives up to the claim. Asefi's responses encapsulated the problem with Iran's political reformists. They wanted to liberalize Iran, allow greater individual freedoms within the context of an Islamic republic, but

they wouldn't take effective action against those who broke the law and undercut the positive reforms.

But the people of Iran aren't relying on politicians to make change. Slowly, and sometimes in small ways, Iranians are rebelling against the tight strictures that once bound them to a reactionary version of Islam.

The Creeping Dress Codes

From the time of the revolution until the early 1990s, the government required women to wear a manteau or the all-encompassing chador. The chador is a full-length cloth cut into a semicircle and wrapped around the body and head. It is the traditional Iranian hijab, or "cover" for women. Translated literally, *chador* means "tent." A manteau looks just like a cloth raincoat and comes in various lengths.

According to Islamic teachings, women should be modest and cover themselves while in public. But the type of covering varies widely depending on the country and culture. Saudi Arabian and Afghan women cover themselves head to toe, without even their eyes visible. Some Muslim women in Lebanon wear stylish suits and matching head scarves with the scarves pushed well back, revealing a lot of hair.

Iranian clerics, all men, mandated a very conservative interpretation of the dress code in the early years of the revolution. Unmarried couples couldn't even attend a party together. Film director Jafar Panahi skewered this type of government repression in his excellent 2003 film *Crimson Gold*. In one scene a delivery man on a motorbike brings a pizza to an upscale apartment building in Tehran. He discovers men arresting unmarried couples leaving a party.

Male Policeman: Come out here.

Man with Woman: What's going on? But we're married. Let me
  explain.

Policeman: Yeah, right. Who goes out with his wife?

But rebellion from below gradually forced the government to loosen its policies. By the time of President Khatami's
election in 1997, authorities had all but given up trying to enforce those moral codes inside people's homes. Even ultraconservative President Ahmadinejad hasn't been able to roll back
most of the reforms from the 90s.

One day I visited an upscale shopping mall in north Tehran.
Wealthy Iranians wandered through stores stocked with imported cosmetics, Italian designer clothes, and hi-tech sound
systems. In a cell phone store, I met fifteen-year-old Michelle
and her mom shopping for a new cell phone. Michelle had the
unfortunate habit of losing her cell phone, and they were bargaining for an inexpensive replacement.

Michelle's mom was wearing a head scarf and manteau.
Michelle was wearing a head scarf, sandals, jeans, and a green
manteau about the length of a long shirt. "When we bought
the manteau, it was up to here," said mom, pointing to her
daughter's mid calf. "But we shortened it." In the United
States, teens like to wear short skirts, and the shortening urge
is apparently international. "It's more stylish," said Michelle
with a big grin.

Then I asked about a more controversial topic. Does Michelle
ever go to parties? The resulting dialogue was revealing.

Michelle: Yes, of course.

Mom: But only girls.

Michelle: No! Not these days.

Mom: Maybe brothers of a couple of girls.

Michelle: No, Mom! We go to parties. There are boys. We hang
out. [giggling] Mommy![13]

When the boys and girls get a little older, the parties get a
lot wilder. At several north Tehran parties I attended, people
not only drank alcohol but smoked hashish and even snorted
coke. I was more worried about a police raid than they were. (I
could see the next day's headline: "American spy found con-
sorting with drug-crazed teens and unaccompanied women.")

By far the most popular illegal activity behind closed doors
is watching satellite TV. The government has tried to stop
news and entertainment from the outside world. And it has
failed.

Satellite TV—Now You See It, Now You Don't

The satellite TV revolution hit the Middle East in the 1990s.
For the first time, people of the region could see timely news
and entertainment shows banned on state-run TV. People
were fascinated with everything from English-language news
on BBC or CNN to videos of scantily clad belly dancers un-
dulating on screen.

The Iranian government first tried to prohibit satellite
dishes in 1995, and it has waged a largely unsuccessful effort
to enforce the ban ever since. Satellite dish prices have
dropped. In 2006, friends in Iran told me you could buy a
satellite dish and descrambler for $100. Most stations are pi-
rated, so viewers don't pay monthly fees. The dishes are af-
fordable to middle-income and even some working-class
Iranians.

I sat down one evening and counted over 500 channels
available on the Hotbird satellite, including foreign news

broadcasts, American film channels, and even pornography. The vast majority of sites seemed to be Arabic music video stations, judging from the women dancing and lip synching on screen. But over a dozen channels broadcast in Farsi, including the Voice of America and some Los Angeles–based Iranian exile stations.

After Mahmoud Ahmadinejad was elected president in 2005, he tried yet another crackdown. Police using helicopters and airplanes located satellite dishes on rooftops. Then the police went to each building, demanding that the dishes come down and forcing residents to pay a fine.

But residents didn't miss their favorite programs for very long. The system is so corrupt that sometimes a simple bribe allowed the dishes to remain pointing skyward. In other cases, residents were more creative. One journalist friend told me how the police came to his building and took away the forest of dishes. But since he was a foreign reporter, he was legally entitled to keep his. So all the neighbors hooked up their cables to his dish, and he is now the most popular guy in the building. Another friend took his satellite dish off the roof and placed it on his balcony.

The dishes and descramblers are imported from abroad, often with the assistance of corrupt officials. Some Revolutionary Guard leaders get a cut from the illicit smuggling of satellite dishes, liquor, and drugs.

The underground economy functions rather efficiently. Friends wanting liquor one night simply called a local bootlegger, who delivered a variety of name-brand bottles that evening. When I visited a private apartment in Tehran, the satellite system suddenly stopped working. The owner went up on the roof but couldn't figure out the problem. He called the satellite man, who came out within two hours and replaced the receiver immediately. I can't get that kind of service at home in Oakland.

A Memorable Trip

Sean, Norman, and I visited Iran in June 2005 during the country's tumultuous presidential election. In August Sean published a five-part series in the *San Francisco Chronicle* that amassed one of the highest numbers of online readers in the paper's history.[14] The articles were translated, e-mailed, and posted on blogs all over Iran.

On our first day in Tehran, we interviewed some people at a coffeehouse. Afterwards, all the customers cleared out and went out front to take cell phone pictures with Sean. One of those images got e-mailed to friends, who forwarded it to friends until it became like a Hollywood chain letter. One of my friends got twenty copies of the e-mail from different people. Sean's trip became headline news every day, and dozens of fans camped out in the hotel lobby, hoping to get an autograph.

When I returned to Iran in November 2006, I assumed our trip had been quickly forgotten, one of those blips on the celebrity radar. In numerous spontaneous discussions, however, people asked proudly if I knew that Sean Penn had visited Iran. They would then launch into a detailed description of his trip, which I didn't have the heart to correct in any way.

Sean's articles, an excellent introduction to Iran for Americans, showed the nature of the ruling dictatorship. They showed how every day, sometimes in little ways, Iranians express their discontent with the system. At the same time,

Iranians reject U.S. plans to "help build democracy in Iran" and certainly oppose any U.S. military action against their country.

Former ambassador Freeman likened U.S. policy to someone with mental illness. "A psychotic thinks that $2 + 2 = 5$," he told me. "But a neurotic knows that $2 + 2 = 4$, but he's very unhappy about it. Washington falls in the neurotic category, unwilling to accept reality happily."[15]

These days the neuroses begin when U.S. officials look at Iran's nuclear program.

TWO

United States Tells Iran: Become a Nuclear Power

Top Democratic and Republican leaders absolutely believe that Iran is planning to develop nuclear weapons. And one of their seemingly strongest arguments involves a process of deduction. Since Iran has so much oil, they argue, why develop nuclear power?

James Woolsey typifies the view. The director of the CIA under both George Bush (the elder) and Bill Clinton said, "There is no underlying reason for one of the greatest oil producers in the world to need to get into the nuclear [energy] business . . . unless what they want to do is train and produce people and an infrastructure that can have highly enriched uranium or plutonium, fissionable material for nuclear weapons."[1]

In an op-ed commentary, former secretary of state Henry Kissinger wrote, "For a major oil producer such as Iran, nuclear energy is a wasteful use of resources," a position later cited approvingly by the Bush administration.[2]

But U.S. leaders are engaging in a massive case of collective amnesia, or perhaps more accurately, intentional misdirection. In the 1970s the United States encouraged Iran to develop nuclear power precisely because Iran will eventually run out of oil.

A declassified document from President Gerald Ford's administration, for which Kissinger was secretary of state, supported Iran's push for nuclear power. The document noted that Tehran should "prepare against the time—about 15 years in the future—when Iranian oil production is expected to decline sharply."[3]

The United States ultimately planned to sell billions of dollars' worth of nuclear reactors, spare parts, and nuclear fuel to Iran. Muhammad Sahimi, a professor and former department chair of the Chemical and Petroleum Engineering Department at the University of Southern California, told me that Kissinger thought "it was in the U.S. national interest, both economic and security interest, to have such close relations in terms of nuclear power."[4]

The shah even periodically hinted that he wanted Iran to build nuclear weapons. In June 1974, the shah proclaimed that Iran would have nuclear weapons "without a doubt and sooner than one would think."[5] Iranian embassy officials in France later denied the shah made those remarks, and the shah disowned them. But a few months later, the shah noted that Iran "has no intention of acquiring nuclear weapons but if small states began building them, then Iran might have to reconsider its policy."[6]

If an Iranian leader made such statements today, the United States and Israel would denounce them as proof of nefarious intent. They might well threaten military action if Iran didn't immediately halt its nuclear buildup. At the time, however, the comments caused no ripples in Washington or Tel Aviv because the shah was a staunch ally of both. Asked to comment on his contradictory views then and now, Kissinger said, "They were an allied country, and this was a commercial transaction. We didn't address the question of them one day moving toward nuclear weapons."[7]

Kissinger should have added that consistency has never been a strong point of U.S. foreign policy.

Nukes and Party-Mad Dictators

To fully understand the hypocrisy of U.S. foreign policy, we must travel back to the era of bell-bottoms, funny-looking polyester shirts, and party-mad dictators.

In the early 1970s, Iran's repressive dictator was perhaps most famous for his prodigious partying. In October 1971, Shah Mohammed Reza Pahlavi celebrated the 2,500th anniversary of the Persian empire with a lavish, three-day party on the site of the ancient city of Persepolis. Luminaries such as Vice President Spiro Agnew, Britain's Prince Philip, and Ethiopian dictator Haile Selassie consumed twenty-five thousand bottles of French wine, five thousand bottles of champagne, and massive quantities of caviar flown in by Maxim's of Paris. Iran's per capita income was only $350 per year; the party cost an estimated $100 million.[8] The excesses of the party helped fuel anger against the shah at home and abroad.

But in those days, successive U.S. presidential administrations were tickled pink with the shah's regime. As far as the United States was concerned, the shah had a stable government that was modernizing an economically and religiously backward society. True, he ran a brutal dictatorship unconstrained by elections or an independent judiciary. The National Security and Intelligence Organization (SAVAK), his secret police, was infamous for torturing and murdering political dissidents. But the shah made sure that Iran provided a steady supply of petroleum to U.S. and other Western oil companies. He had his own regional ambitions and also acted as a gendarme for the United States.

Need an ally for Israel in the surrounding Arab world? The shah entered into military and intelligence agreements with the Israelis starting in 1958. Got a rebellion in the Gulf state of Oman? In the early 1970s, the shah sent three thousand troops to put down the leftist rebels[9] and to ensure the region's oil fields remained safe for him and the United States. Iran became America's single biggest arms buyer. It bought $18.1 billion worth of U.S. arms from 1950 to 1977.[10]

U.S. anticommunist diplomacy, military expansion, and business profit all melded together nicely. And that's where nuclear power comes in.

Beginning in the late 1960s, the shah began to worry about Iran's long-term electric energy supplies. Iran had fewer than five hundred thousand electricity consumers in 1963, but those numbers swelled to over two million in 1976.[11] The shah worried that Iran's oil deposits would eventually run out and that burning petroleum for electricity would waste an important resource. He could earn far more exporting oil than using it for power generation.

Hermidas Bavand, second in command of Iran's Mission to the United Nations under the shah and now a professor of international law at Allameh Tabatabaee University in Tehran, told me that the position of the shah on nuclear power was almost identical to that of the current Iranian government. Back then, proponents of nuclear power said Iran had to prepare for the day when the oil runs out. Secondly, said Bavand,

"Iran had to keep up with scientific and technological" progress in the world. And Iran craved international prestige. Bavand said, "Many countries—Brazil, Argentina, Israel— were developing nuclear energy. So they thought that Iran should have nuclear power" as well.[12]

Successive Republican and Democratic administrations in the United States backed the shah's elaborate plans to make nuclear power an integral part of Iran's electrical grid, in no small part because he would buy a lot of his nuclear equipment from the USA.

The United States established Iran's first research reactor in 1967 at the University of Tehran. In November of that year, the U.S. corporation United Nuclear provided Iran with 5.85 kilograms of 93 percent enriched uranium.[13]

By the 1970s, nuclear power was becoming increasingly unpopular in the United States and around the world, as hundreds of thousands of people marched and blockaded nuclear facilities. Even before the Three Mile Island and Chernobyl disasters, the antinuclear movement pointed out that many reactors were unsafe. In addition, the industry had no long-term, secure method for transporting and storing nuclear waste produced at the reactors. Massive demonstrations and rising costs meant U.S. nuclear power companies were having a hard time getting permits to build reactors. Eventually, the permitting process stopped altogether.

Permits never seemed to be a problem in Iran, however. In 1974, Richard Helms, then U.S. Ambassador to Iran and later head of the CIA, wrote to Shah Mohammad Reza Pahlavi, "We have noted the priority that His Imperial Majesty gives to developing alternative means of energy production through nuclear power. This is clearly an area in which we might most usefully begin on a specific program of cooperation and collaboration."

Helms went on to write, "The Secretary [of State Henry Kissinger] has asked me to underline emphatically the seriousness of our purpose and our desire to move forward vigorously in appropriate ways."[14]

General Electric and Westinghouse ultimately won contracts to build eight reactors in Iran. By the time of the Iranian revolution in 1979, the shah had plans to buy a total of eighteen nuclear power reactors from the United States, France, and Germany.[15]

Evidence has emerged since the 1979 Iranian revolution that the shah did more than make embarrassing public references to building nuclear weapons. Documents show that Israel and Iran had discussed modification of Israel's Jericho missiles, which could have been fitted with nuclear warheads.[16] A research report from the Nuclear Threat Initiative, an organization founded by conservative Democrat and former senator Sam Nunn, explained that the shah was suspected of experimenting with nuclear weapons design, plutonium extraction and laser-enrichment research.[17]

Nuclear expert Sahimi argued that presidents Nixon and Ford "would not have minded if the shah developed the Bomb because the shah was a close ally of the United States. Remember, Iran had a long border with the Soviet Union. If the shah did make a nuclear bomb, that would have been a big deterrent against the USSR."[18]

Neither Sahimi nor other experts say the shah had actually developed a nuclear bomb. But the United States denounces the current Iranian government for activity at least as suspicious as that carried out by the shah.

Since the United States wasn't terribly concerned about an

Iranian Bomb in the 1970s, it also wasn't worried about Iran's enriching its own uranium. The United States gave approval when the shah bought a 25 percent stake in a French company making enriched uranium. But the shah wanted to build enrichment facilities inside Iran, as well. No country wants to be reliant on others for fuel whose absence could shut down a portion of its electricity grid. The United States actually encouraged Iran to enrich its own uranium.[19]

Today when Iran demands that it be able to enrich uranium for nuclear power purposes, under strict international supervision, the United States says that's proof Iran wants to develop nuclear weapons.

Mohamed ElBaradei, the Consummate Inspector

Mohamed ElBaradei looks every inch the international diplomat. The Egyptian keeps his shoes shined and suits sharply pressed. Glasses and a balding pate give him the look of authority. Indeed, he has steered the International Atomic Energy Agency (IAEA) through very troubled waters in recent years. Prior to the U.S. invasion of Iraq in 2003, ElBaradei correctly said Saddam Hussein did not have a nuclear weapons program. In retaliation, the Bush administration tried to block his reelection to head the IAEA. ElBaradei gathered widespread international support, however, and beat back administration efforts. He won reelection to his post at the end of 2005.

Oh, and did I mention that he and the IAEA won the Nobel Peace Prize in 2005?

I was on the phone from Oakland when ElBaradei entered the radio studio at the UN headquarters in New York to be interviewed by Walter Cronkite for a radio documentary I was producing about nuclear weapons. I was surprised that El-Baradei expressed an almost teenage giddiness about being in the presence of Cronkite.

"It is an honor to be here with you, Mr. Cronkite. I watched your news broadcasts for many years as a young man."[20]

There was something special about listening to these two eminent authorities in their fields. Cronkite had long reported on nuclear issues and was very concerned about nuclear weapons proliferation. When Cronkite asked ElBaradei about Iran, the answer was succinct.

"Some people suspect [the Iranians] have the intention to develop a nuclear weapon," said ElBaradei. "This is a matter of concern to us. But this is not [an] imminent threat."

ElBaradei, unlike successive U.S. administrations, bases his conclusions on facts unearthed through analysis of data and on-the-ground inspections. As a signer of the Non-Proliferation Treaty (NPT), Iran followed the treaty requirements to allow IAEA inspectors into its nuclear facilities. ElBaradei has criticized the Iranian government for lack of transparency and restricting some access in recent years. But ElBaradei has never accused Iran of planning to make a nuclear weapon.

So if the guy in charge of inspecting nuclear sites says he has no proof Iran is developing the Bomb, why are so many people in the United States convinced that it is? For that understanding, we'll have to go back to the years just after the Iranian revolution of 1979.

Is Nuclear Power Islamic?

Shortly after coming to power, Iran's Supreme Leader Ayatollah Ruhollah Khomeini scrapped the shah's nuclear power programs as un-Islamic. In fact, he called nuclear power "the work of the devil."[21]

Not coincidentally, the United States and Europeans had completely halted their devil's work in Iran. Germany had stopped construction on the Bushehr nuclear reactor. The United States, Germany, and France had cut off supplies of equipment and nuclear material. All three governments had refused to refund any money already paid, despite cancellation of the nuclear contracts. So while Koranic scholars might disagree on whether nuclear power was consistent with Islam, as a practical matter, Iran wasn't getting any.

Starting in 1980, Iran fought a bloody war with Iraq. Each side feared the other might develop nuclear weapons. Iraq repeatedly bombed Iran's unfinished nuclear facilities, further setting back any possibility of completing them.

By the end of the war in 1988, Iran was in the midst of a population explosion. Iran's population grew from 39.2 million in 1980 to 68.7 million in 2006. Iran's energy planners could see that demand would far outstrip supply. Continuing to extract oil and natural gas at the projected levels wouldn't be enough to guarantee a steady supply of electricity.[22] An analysis by a National Academy of Sciences scientist predicted Iran could run out of oil to export by 2015.[23]

So nuclear power was back on the table. In 1989 Iranian President Akbar Hashemi Rafsanjani signed a ten-point agreement with the USSR to provide nuclear materials and related equipment. The Soviets were to finish the Bushehr reactor started by the Germans in the 1970s. In 1990 Iran signed a ten-year nuclear cooperation agreement with China.

Although it was kept secret at the time, Iran also bought parts and technology from A. Q. Khan, Pakistan's so-called father of the atomic bomb, who also had nuclear dealings with Libya and North Korea. Iran built a secret nuclear facility in the central Iranian city of Natanz. Later, after three years of inspections, the IAEA also determined that Iran had used lasers to purify uranium starting in 1991 and had researched a rare element called polonium-210, which could be used in a nuclear bomb trigger.[24]

The Iranians argued that they had engaged in the secret activity to prevent the United States from stopping their plans for nuclear power development and that they had no intention of developing nuclear weapons.

Discussing the issue of secrecy, Sahimi told me, "Let's say Iran had announced back in 1985 that 'Hey guys, we want to make a uranium enrichment facility.' What do you think would have happened? Would the U.S. and [European Union] have rushed to help Iran? No, they would have done everything in their power to deny Iran's rights."[25]

In 2003 Supreme Leader Ayatollah Ali Khamenei issued a fatwa, an official religious ruling, that declared Islam forbids the building or stockpiling of nuclear weapons.[26] Before dismissing such a ruling as propaganda, it's worth noting that similar religious reasoning stopped Iran from using chemical weapons during the Iran-Iraq War, despite Saddam Hussein's numerous chemical assaults against Iranian troops and civilians.

Enriching Uranium—a Tough Rock to Crack

The United States asserts that Iran's desire to enrich uranium demonstrates its desire to develop nuclear weapons. So what is enrichment anyway?

Raw uranium must go through a process to raise the concentration of the isotope U-235 in order to either produce fuel for a nuclear reactor or make a nuclear bomb. Despite twenty years of off-and-on attempts, Iran has yet to perfect the process on any industrial scale.

Iran does have a limited amount of domestic uranium. First, the ore would have to be milled and subjected to an acid bath to leech out the uranium. The resulting yellowish ore is called yellow cake. Then it's combined with fluorine to produce uranium hexafluoride, or UF6.

Then the process gets really hairy. The uranium hexafluoride must pass through a series of hundreds of spinning centrifuges. Imagine a bunch of pipes and whirling motors passing the liquid through cascading cylinders like a water filtration system.[27]

The cascades can produce 5 percent enriched U-235 for use in nuclear power plants. Iran would have to make 93 percent enriched uranium to make a nuclear bomb but can do so using the same technical process. By the summer of 2007, Iran had installed 1300 centrifuges. But it needs an estimated 3000 centrifuges running flawlessly for a year to make one nuclear bomb.

And getting those centrifuge cascades to work properly is a big technical challenge, according to experts. The centrifuges "spin 60,000 rounds per minute," said Sahimi. "They generate a lot of vibrations, which must be controlled. The centrifuges can't be contaminated because they are easily corroded. Once the centrifuges start working, it's not wise to shut them down and start them again. This damages them. There are all sorts of technical problems."

In August 2006 the IAEA reported that Iran had to slow down its enrichment activities, perhaps due to technical difficulties with the centrifuges.[28] ElBaradei said in October 2006, that even with all of Iran's centrifuges running, it would take years to enrich enough uranium to make a single Bomb.[29]

Iran Is Just Five to Ten Years from Making a Bomb, Really

Every few years U.S. intelligence officials estimate Iran is just years from making a Bomb. In 1995, a "senior U.S. official" estimated Iran was five years from making the Bomb.[30] A 2005 National Intelligence Estimate, representing a consensus among U.S. intelligence agencies, predicted Iran could have the Bomb somewhere around 2015.[31] In early 2006 Israeli intelligence, on the other hand, argued that Iran is much closer to having a Bomb, perhaps one to three years away. In citing such estimates, the U.S. media don't provide any corroboration nor explain why the Israeli assessment differs so widely from the CIA's and IAEA's. Indeed, Israel keeps postponing its estimates of when Iran will have the Bomb. At the end of 2006, Meir Dagan, head of the Mossad intelligence agency, claimed Iran could have a Bomb by 2009 or 2010.[32]

Israel's estimates are clearly influenced by its political and military goals. Using President Mahmoud Ahmadinejad's statements attacking Israel and questioning the existence of the Holocaust, Israel proclaims Iran an immediate military threat. In reality, Ahmadinejad poses no offensive nuclear threat to Israel.[33] Iran would be insane to launch a first strike against the militarily far superior Israel, let alone a nuclear strike with an arsenal of one or two bombs. Such an action would give the United States and Israel a political excuse to wreck havoc on Iran and gain lots of international support.

But Israel does have a vested interest in creating anxiety around a possible Iranian Bomb. While Iran has no ability to wipe Israel off the map, it does support the Palestinian group Hamas and the Lebanese political party and guerrilla group Hizbollah. Iran gives them political, financial, and military backing. Israel doesn't want to suffer another defeat like its 2006 war against Hizbollah. So rather than give up occupied territory and agree to establishing a Palestinian state, Israeli leaders blame outsiders. Israel seeks to weaken or, preferably, overthrow Iran's government.

Israeli officials, along with U.S. hawks, argue that Iran will soon reach "a point of no return," in which it will have both the theoretical knowledge and the practical ability to create weapons-grade plutonium. After that point, the hawks argue, Iran must be confronted militarily. The advantage of this argument, of course, is that it's all hypothetical. The Iranians cross this point of no return at whatever time the hawks allege. Who can prove otherwise?

In the spring of 2006, Bush seemed to echo those sentiments, justifying a military attack by setting the bar impossibly high for Iran. "The world is united and concerned about [Iranians'] desire to have not only a nuclear weapon, but the capacity to make a nuclear weapon or *the knowledge as to how to make a nuclear weapon*" (emphasis added), Bush said in an April 2006 press conference.[34] No one can possibly prove what knowledge scientists might have in their brains. But according to Bush's logic, Iran is a dangerous enemy so long as its scientists might, at some time in the future, think about building a Bomb.

On July 31, 2006, the United States rounded up European powers, and got China and Russia to acquiesce, to pass UN

Security Council Resolution 1696. The resolution demanded that Iran stop "all enrichment-related and reprocessing activities."[35] (Reprocessing involves removing highly radioactive plutonium from nuclear waste products, a procedure that can lead to production of bomb-grade fuel.) A month later, in a report not released to the public, IAEA Director ElBaradei indicated that Iran was *not* reprocessing uranium.

ElBaradei criticized Iran, however, for continued attempts at uranium enrichment. "Iran has not addressed the long outstanding verification issues or provided the necessary transparency to remove uncertainties associated with some of its activities," wrote ElBaradei.[36]

An IAEA official told the *New York Times,* "the qualitative and quantitative development of Iran's enrichment program continues to be fairly limited."[37]

The IAEA report was hardly a smoking gun. But the Bush administration huffed and puffed that Iran's failure to uphold the Security Council resolution meant the world should impose more sanctions. On March 24, 2007, the UN Security Council voted to impose another round of sanctions, prohibiting the sale of Iranian weapons to other countries and freezing the overseas assets of more Iranian individuals and organizations.

The United States failed to get any backing for military attacks on Iran to enforce the sanctions. The March resolution even restated the UN position that the Middle East region should be nuclear free, a criticism of Israel's large nuclear arsenal.

U.S. officials told the *New York Times* that the new sanctions went beyond the nuclear issue. "The new language was written to rein in what [U.S. officials] see as Tehran's ambitions to become the dominant military power in the Persian Gulf and across the Middle East."[38]

Apparently, no one can hold that job except the United States.

No Nukes? Not Enough

The real dispute between the United States and Iran has little to do with Iran's ability to develop nuclear weapons. The Bush administration declared Iran to be part of the "axis of evil" and has been pursuing a policy of "regime change," a euphemism for the U.S. overthrow of an internationally recognized government. The United States has adopted different tactical positions, sometimes calling for a tightening of sanctions, other times threatening military strikes. But the long-term goal is installation of a friendly regime.

The American people now know that the Bush administration lied about weapons of mass destruction in Iraq in 2003. But back then, the threat of WMDs served as a powerful argument to convince Americans of the need for regime change. The phony nuclear weapons issue plays precisely the same role in U.S. plans for Iran.

Iran's Supreme Leader Khamenei said the United States "has used nuclear energy as an excuse. If Iran quits now, the case will not be over. The Americans will find another excuse."[39]

Let's say Iran stopped all nuclear programs tomorrow and that was verified by international inspectors. The United States could start a new campaign based on its current claim that Iran is "the most active sponsor of state terrorism" in the world.[40] Iran could give terrorist groups chemical weapons. Iran has missiles capable of hitting Tel Aviv and U.S. military bases in the Middle East. Iran presents an immediate danger because of its support for terrorism. Time for regime change.

Is Iran currently developing nuclear weapons? No. Could it do so sometime in the future? Sure. According to ElBaradei, some forty-nine countries "now know how to make nuclear arms," including Japan, South Korea, and other U.S. allies. Neither the United States nor the UN Security Council can militarily prevent each of those countries from making a Bomb, said ElBaradei. "We are relying primarily on the continued good intentions of these countries, intentions which are in turn based on their sense of security."[41]

The only way to ensure Iran doesn't make nuclear weapons is to devise a political, not a military, solution. If the people of Iran have a government that truly represents them, and the United States ceases its hostility and negotiates in good faith, Iran won't see a need to develop nuclear weapons.

So What Would You Do?

When I speak at college campuses and before community groups, someone inevitably asks me a legitimate question: "OK, U.S. policy toward Iran's nuclear program is wrong. If you were president, what would you do?" Glad you asked.

First, no more demonizing Iran. I would apologize for years of U.S. aggression against Iran. I would offer to return the billions of dollars in illegally frozen Iranian assets now held by the United States, lift all existing sanctions against Iran, and offer to restore full diplomatic relations.[42] That would get Iran's attention. More important, it would set the basis for easing tensions on issues such as nuclear weapons.

I would announce plans to reduce the unconscionable

number of nuclear weapons maintained by the United States in violation of the Non-Proliferation Treaty. Most Americans have no idea that the Non-Proliferation Treaty not only limits other states from obtaining nuclear weapons but also requires disarmament by the existing nuclear states, including the United States.[43]

Then I would do something neither side expects. I would tell them we will phase out our nuclear power reactors for safety reasons and because we can't safely store nuclear waste. Nuclear power plants in the United States aren't even hardened against an airplane crash, and the Nuclear Regulatory Commission refuses to require it.

Then I would suggest that Iran not develop nuclear power. Nuclear reactors and their tons of radioactive waste are disasters waiting to happen. Iran is already planning to have 20 percent of its electricity supplied by hydropower by 2021. Iran has the potential to develop a lot more wind and geothermal power as well.[44] In the meantime Iran could harness its tremendous natural gas resources as a relatively efficient source of electricity generation.

I don't know how Iranian leaders would react. These suggestions would certainly spark a lot of discussion among Iranians, a debate now largely nonexistent.[45] Journalist and opposition leader Akbar Ganji is one of the few Iranians I met concerned about the safety of nuclear plants. "I am very worried that something like Chernobyl will happen to Iran," he told me. "If that happens, the Iranian people will pay the heaviest price."[46]

I would like to see Ganji's views prevail. But if, after a genuine debate, Iranians decided they wanted nuclear power, so be it.

The IAEA has procedures that allow countries to develop nuclear power, subject to strict international inspection. On March 23, 2005, Iran offered a plan to Britain, France, and Germany that would have allowed Iran to develop nuclear power and engage in uranium enrichment. Iran agreed not to reprocess nuclear fuel, to produce only low-enriched uranium, to limit the number of centrifuges, and to guarantee on-site inspections by the IAEA.[47] That proposal could serve as the basis for honest negotiations.

Should the world simply trust Iran's leaders? No. We don't have to assume good faith. The IAEA is quite capable of detecting NPT violations, because radioactive particles inevitably show up in water and soil. Over a period of time, and allowed full access, the IAEA can detect illegal nuclear activity. Since even U.S. intelligence agencies agree Iran is many years from building a Bomb, why not allow the IAEA to do its job?

In the long run, the people of Iran must change their government and revisit the nuclear power issue. I hope they choose to develop safer forms of energy. But that's a decision to be made by the people of Iran, not rulers in Washington.

THREE

Iran, Hizbollah, and Israel: The Real Story

What I remember most clearly about Eliahu Ben-Elissar was his goatee. It wasn't just any goatee. It resembled an elegant, carefully trimmed shaving brush. The goatee descended directly from the great European facial hair of the early 1900s.

When I met Ben-Elissar in Jerusalem back in 1987, he was a ranking member of the Knesset (parliament) foreign affairs committee and a former ambassador to Egypt. Ben-Elissar later became the Israeli ambassador to the United States and died in 2000. But in 1987 he welcomed me into his house on a quiet Jerusalem street and offered coffee. The hospitality matched the goatee.

Ben-Elissar assumed that, as an American Jew, I would be sympathetic to Israel's current policies. Once the pleasantries were over, however, our differences became quite clear. Ben-Elissar strongly advocated hard-right views as a leader of the then-ruling Likud party. Right-winger Yitzhak Shamir was prime minister, and Ben-Elissar reflected Shamir's views. Israel opposed establishing a Palestinian state, claiming that

Palestinians already had their own state, Jordan. Ben-Elissar favored annexing the West Bank. He justified torture by Shin Bet, the Israeli intelligence agency.

But Ben-Elissar took what seemed to be an incongruous position on Iran. He defended Israeli government support of Iran in the Iran-Iraq War. Top Iranian leaders opposed the existence of the Jewish state and regularly spewed anti-Jewish rhetoric. Yet Israel sold spare parts and other arms to Iran. Israel was an integral part of the Iran-Contra scandal, providing arms to both Iran and the Contras in Nicaragua.[1]

Ben-Elissar admitted to me that "the decision to sell arms to Iran was made in secret by [Israel's] prime minister, minister of defense, and foreign minister."[2]

Ben-Elissar explained that Israel considered Iraq the more-dangerous enemy. He said Ayatollah Ruhollah "Khomeini is full of anti-Israeli rhetoric, but that's all." Israel "would not like to see Iran completely defeated because this would make . . . Iraq a big winner."[3]

U.S. congressional investigations confirmed what Ben-Elissar told me that day. The United States had been the main arms supplier to Iran before 1979, and the new clerical government desperately needed to restock its arsenal. Israel had many of the same U.S. weapons, such as TOW and HAWK missiles, as well as spare parts for jet fighters. In its chronology of the Iran-Contra scandal, the National Security Archive wrote, "Iran badly wanted what Israel could provide. . . . Since Israel had those weapons in its inventory, . . . Israel was more than happy to provide those weapons to Iran."[4]

Why would Israel support the rabidly anti-Zionist government in Iran?

Israel had been a close ally of Shah Mohammad Reza

Pahlavi almost to the moment of his overthrow. Israel has a policy of supporting non-Arab governments in the region as a wedge against Arabs. Thus Israel had supported Iran, Turkey, and Ethiopia. So Israel saw no contradiction in supporting the clerical government of Iran despite its frequent and public calls for "Death to Israel."

Yitzhak Rabin, Israeli prime minister from 1974 to 1977 and then again from 1992 to 1995, told a 1987 press conference, "Iran is Israel's best friend, and we do not intend to change our position in relation to Tehran, because Khomeini's regime will not last forever."[5]

But times have changed, and Israel now seeks to demonize Iran rather than Iraq.

Does Iran Want to Kill the Jews?

Shimon Peres said in a speech that President Mahmoud Ahmadinejad "is the only person in the world calling for the annihilation of another people." Peres is a former Labor Party prime minister and deputy prime minister in Ehud Olmert's government. "We need to expose his real face, which is just like Hitler, to the world. . . . Here we have a man with a dangerous personality, just like Hitler, who wants to build dangerous weapons. These kinds of threats we hear from Ahmadinejad have not been heard since Hitler."[6]

Well, actually, Israel's supporters make that claim all the time. The Hitler analogy has been made against Saddam Hussein, Palestine Liberation Organization (PLO) chairman Yasser Arafat, Egypt's President Anwar Sadat (before he signed a peace treaty with Israel), and many other leaders opposed to Israeli policies.[7] In reality, Ahmadinejad is no Hitler, if for no other reason than Iran is no Germany. Both the United States and Israel intentionally distort his words for maximum negative impact. On the other hand, some people in the Muslim world idealize Ahmadinejad as a hero, a reputation he clearly doesn't deserve.

At various times Ahmadinejad has been quoted as saying "Israel must be wiped off the map." In reality, according to several Farsi speakers I consulted, Ahmadinejad is quoting an old slogan from Ayatollah Ruhollah Khomeini that means "this regime occupying Jerusalem must vanish from the page of time." That phrase does not imply Iranian military action against Israel.

But Ahmadinejad really angered world opinion by holding a conference in December 2006 to question the existence of the Holocaust. The conference was a political disaster for Ahmadinejad and led some members of the Majlis to criticize him. A group of a hundred leading Iranian intellectuals, inside and outside Iran, denounced the conference as a "distortion of historical facts."

Ahmadinejad's statements and actions indicate he is profoundly wrong about Jewish history and current Middle East politics. His rhetoric harms the Palestinian people, providing the United States and Israel easy propaganda points. But neither Ahmadinejad nor other major political leaders call for annihilating the Jews.[8]

Ahmadinejad and some other Iranian leaders advocate a one-state solution to the Israeli-Palestinian conflict.[9] All the estimated five million Palestinians now living in exile should return home, Ahmadinejad said in a *Time* magazine interview, "and then the entire people of those lands [will] hold a referendum and choose their own system of government. This is a democratic and popular way."[10]

All the people of those lands includes Muslims, Jews, and Christians. Such a position would eliminate Israel as a Jewish state and would never be accepted by Israelis. The one-state solution was rejected over twenty years ago by the Palestine Liberation Organization and later in a formal Arab League peace plan adopted in 2002 at its summit in Beirut.[11] Palestinians and Arabs continue to believe in a two-state solution, in which a Palestinian state would coexist side by side with the Israeli state. Israel would have to return occupied Arab land and agree to recognize a viable Palestinian nation. In return, Palestinians and Arab states would recognize and live in peace with Israel.

Hamas, which won the 2006 parliamentary elections in the Palestinian Authority, does not accept a two-state solution. However, it does call for a ten-year cease-fire during which it would stop all military attacks on Israel and negotiate peace.[12] I strongly believe that popular opinion and Mideast realities will force Hamas and other rejectionists to eventually change their position.

What gets lost in all the rhetoric, however, is that Ahmadinejad's view is hardly new among Iranian religious leaders. Some top clerics in Iran, including the late Ayatollah Khomeini, have advocated the one-state solution since the 1979 revolution. "This regime occupying Jerusalem must vanish from the page of time" has been scrawled on the side of the U.S. Embassy in Iran since the 1979 hostage crisis. Religious leaders have continually shouted "Death to Israel" at rallies.

In practical terms, Israel faces no greater threat from Iran today than it did back in the 1980s. The rhetoric of President Ahmadinejad remains fiercely anti-Zionist, but Israeli leaders know Iran doesn't have a nuclear bomb. If Iran ever launched an offensive attack on Israel, let alone a nuclear attack, the

Iranian government would be isolated at home and internationally. The United States and Israel would destroy Iran in counterattacks.

"To drop a bomb on Israel is something so insane, it is beyond any pale," Avner Cohen, senior research scholar at the Center for International Security Studies, University of Maryland, told the *Wall Street Journal*.[13]

Ahmadinejad and Iran's rulers are angry, not insane.

Israel doesn't have to worry about an offensive first strike, but if Iran ever did develop nuclear weapons, the United States and Israel would have a much harder time attacking Iran. They would have to calculate whether Iran would use its nuclear arsenal in self-defense. Israeli leaders' scaremongering about Iran's nuclear threat hides their real agenda. Iran supports Lebanon's Hizbollah and the Palestinian group Hamas. Israel seeks to weaken or eliminate those groups. It argues that without the outside support of Iran and, to a lesser extent, Syria, those two groups would no longer pose a threat to Israel.

That argument has a familiar ring. Israel has always blamed the indigenous resistance on outsiders. In the early 1970s, the Israeli government argued that the PLO survived only because of support in Jordan. After it was driven from Jordan in 1971, the PLO survived only because of its bases in Lebanon. When Israel invaded and occupied southern Lebanon and expelled the PLO in 1982, the outside threat became Syria and Iraq. But somehow opposition to Israeli occupation continued to grow. Now the outside agitator is Iran.

Outsiders are not the cause of Palestinian or Lebanese resistance. Military might cannot guarantee Israel's security. Israel must resolve the Palestinian issue and return occupied

Arab land. If the Palestinians agree to a two-state settlement, the views of Iran, Syria, or any other country become irrelevant.

Is Hizbollah a Terrorist Organization?

But what about Lebanon? Should the world be worried about Iran's influence there?

Back in 2003 I wanted to visit the headquarters of Hizbollah in Beirut, but it wasn't easy. The problem was not security. Rather, I was stumped by Beirut's confusing system of addresses. For many Shiite neighborhoods, you drive to the general location and then ask a passerby for the specific destination. This works great for locals but can be a problem for someone who doesn't speak Arabic.

"Don't worry," Haidar Dikmak, Hizbollah chief press officer, told me over the phone, "any taxi driver will know how to get you here." He was right. I told the grizzled old man driving my taxi to take me to the Hizbollah offices. We arrived about thirty minutes later, after stopping to ask a passerby, of course.

Many Americans have an image of Hizbollah as a group of wild-eyed terrorists with their turbans in a twist. In reality, Hizbollah has become the most popular Shia Muslim political party in Lebanon. In 2005 Hizbollah elected fourteen members to parliament and joined the cabinet. Hizbollah has garnered support by operating hospitals, schools, and social service agencies. On the other hand, it has a fundamentalist vision for the future of Lebanon, takes a hard line against Israel, and maintains its own guerrilla army.

Even American diplomats, when speaking off the record,

downplayed the official terrorism designation. One U.S. official in Beirut in June 2003 told me the United States still considers Hizbollah an enemy but said the group had changed significantly. "No one in Lebanon thinks Hizbollah is a terrorist organization. We recognize they do social work. They've become more sophisticated in military terms as well as fund-raising and providing services."

Hizbollah is also quite open about its political ties to Iran. Walk down the street in the Shiite districts of Lebanon, and you'll see posters of Hizbollah leader Sheik Hassan Nasrallah, Ayatollah Khomeini, and Iran's current Supreme Leader Sayyed Ali Kamenei. Of course, those bearded visages also decorated the walls of Hizbollah's modest office when I visited.

It was an oppressively hot summer day in Beirut, and the sweat poured down my back as I hiked up the stairs to Dikmak's office. I had traveled to Lebanon on assignment for the *San Francisco Chronicle*. Dikmak's place was the first stop in getting permission to visit Hizbollah-controlled areas of southern Lebanon. In theory, anyone could travel anywhere in Lebanon. But in reality, Hizbollah controlled a sizable swath of Lebanese territory.

I watched with fascination as Dikmak typed the *Chronicle's* name into his computer database. He scanned several articles that staffers and freelancers had written about Hizbollah. Luckily, the most recent visitor had been Robert Collier, a fine *Chronicle* reporter without the usual Middle East ax to grind.

Dikmak had even mastered the mainstream media terminology. "Ah, yes," he said with a slight smile, "Mr. Collier's articles were quite objective." An assistant brought in strong Arabic coffee, and we had an informal chat.

At one point, almost in passing, he mentioned the "Four Mothers." I had no idea who they were. I found out later that the Four Mothers were a group of Israeli women who became famous for organizing against the Israeli occupation of Lebanon, which ended in 2000. Any Israeli would have recognized the reference. Luckily, I did not.

Israel periodically sends spies into Lebanon disguised as journalists. Had I been more familiar with recent Israeli history, I might have been mistaken for an agent, the 007 of Oakland. But seeing as how I was a writer for an objective newspaper and not a spy, I was given permission to visit and interview people in southern Lebanon.

The drive south of Beirut in those days was quite beautiful. The modern highway gave way to winding roads. Spectacular views of the Mediterranean slowly disappeared only to be exchanged for scenic, rolling hills. Much of this land was destroyed in the 2006 Israel-Lebanon War, however, and will take years to completely rebuild.

On the 2003 trip, I eventually drove all the way down to the Lebanese-Israeli border. We stopped at the Fatima Gate, a long-closed border crossing point. Standing on a hill, I could see the developed towns and agricultural fields of Israel. I could also shop at outdoor stands selling tsotchkes to tourists: Hizbollah lapel pins, CDs, flags, and T-shirts. After a bit of haggling, I finally bought a genuine Hizbollah coffee mug.

We drove back up the coast and then inland for a meeting with Mohammed Raad, the head of Hizbollah's parliamentary group. Raad explained that Iran provides political and moral support for Hizbollah. But despite these close ties, he said, Hizbollah makes its own decisions.[14]

Hizbollah emerged in the early 1980s when it split from Amal, the Lebanese Shiite political party and militia. Hizbollah rejected Amal's vaguely leftist political stands and its corruption. Iran played an important role from the beginning, offering political, military, and financial support to Hizbollah. Iranian Revolutionary Guards helped train Hizbollah in the Bekaa Valley of Lebanon and provided financial aid, although neither side has ever revealed the amount. Some years ago, Farid El Khazen, a political science professor at the American University of Beirut, told me he estimated Iran provided $100 million in military and civilian assistance annually.[15] Iran publicly pledged $500 million to Hizbollah during the 2006 war.[16]

Iranian and Hizbollah leaders share a common ideology. Both reject a two-state solution for the Palestinian conflict. Both see a central role for Shia Islam in government. Hizbollah initially favored forming an Islamic state in Lebanon, similar to what exists in Iran. Since the 1990s, however, Hizbollah has recognized that a majority of Lebanese would not support establishment of a Shia Islamic state. So Hizbollah pushes for Islamic rule in areas it controls, without trying to impose that on the entire country.

El Khazen told me, "Ultimately, Hizbollah knows that a country like Lebanon, with so many different communities and sects—Sunni, Shia, Christians—they know it's not easy to establish an Islamic state."

While relations between Iran and Hizbollah are close, Hizbollah remains a nationalist party with its focus on Lebanon. In the long run—after Israel eventually returns occupied land to Lebanon and Syria and resolves the Palestinian issue—Hizbollah must still function as a political party in

Lebanon. That means Hizbollah has no future as a proxy for Iran.

I had the pleasure of working with Iranian journalist and documentary filmmaker Maziar Bahari during my 2000 trip to Iran. He has studied Iran's and Hizbollah's leaders and remains a sharp critic of both. He notes, however, that Hizbollah is no puppet. "Hizbollah, to a great extent, makes decisions independently of Iran," he wrote. "Hizbollah is an indigenous Lebanese armed resistance group that owes it popularity to Israeli atrocities, biased American policies, and corrupt Lebanese politicians. When the United States and Israel try to portray Hizbollah as an Iranian proxy, they are pointing the finger in the wrong direction."[17]

Who Won the 2006 Israel-Lebanon War?

In June 2006, Israel sent troops back into Gaza, after having unilaterally withdrawn in September 2005.[18] Fierce fighting broke out between Palestinians and the Israeli army. In a particularly horrendous incident, Israeli warships shelled a beach in Gaza on June 9, killing seven civilians and wounding fifteen. The chilling images were captured by TV cameras and broadcast around the world. The Israeli government claimed that the people had been killed by Palestinian land mines, but Human Rights Watch investigators held the Israeli navy responsible.[19]

In this context, Hizbollah launched a well-planned raid from Lebanon into northern Israel on July 12. It ambushed Israeli soldiers, killing eight and capturing two. It hoped to exchange the Israeli soldiers for Lebanese prisoners held in Israel. In previous years, Israel had retaliated for border incidents with artillery and air strikes inside Lebanon. Hizbollah leader Nasrallah later said he expected such retaliation once again. But this time the recently elected government of Prime Minister Ehud Olmert decided to pummel Hizbollah into submission with a full-scale air bombardment, followed by a ground invasion. Why adopt such a hard-line policy?

Clearly, Israel wanted to punish Hizbollah, both for its support of the Palestinians and for holding Israeli soldiers captive. But the United States played a strong role as well. In the spring of 2006, the Bush Administration had been ramping up its rhetoric and threatening military strikes against Iran. The United States feared, however, that if it attacked Iran, the clerical government would encourage Hizbollah and Hamas to retaliate. So the United States urged Israel to severely weaken and, if possible, wipe out Hizbollah.

Seymour Hersh wrote in the *New Yorker*:

> The Bush Administration . . . was closely involved in the planning of Israel's retaliatory attacks. President Bush and Vice President Dick Cheney were convinced, current and former intelligence and diplomatic officials told me, that a successful Israeli Air Force bombing campaign against Hizbollah's heavily fortified underground-missile and command-and-control complexes in Lebanon could ease Israel's security concerns and also serve as a prelude to a potential American preemptive attack to destroy Iran's nuclear installations.[20]

Hersh quotes a former senior intelligence officer who characterized Cheney's views. "What if the Israelis . . . [are] really successful? It'd be great. We can learn what to do in Iran by watching what the Israelis do in Lebanon."

Or what not to do.

Hizbollah was a lot better armed and organized than either the United States or Israel imagined. In the first days after Israel's attack, Hizbollah sank an Israeli warship with an Iranian-made C-802 missile, the first such sinking since Israel's founding in 1948. Despite a month of aerial bombardment throughout Lebanon, Hizbollah kept up a daily barrage of Iranian-supplied missiles fired into Israel. Israeli ground troops in Lebanon faced fierce house-to-house combat, including weaponry that destroyed some of their heavily armored tanks.

Israeli aerial bombardments damaged many of Lebanon's bridges, roads, and other infrastructure, including some Lebanese army bases and towns inhabited by Lebanese Christians. Many Christians had sided with Israel in the 1980s, but that apparently didn't matter this time. Israel hoped that the bombardments would force non-Shiite Lebanese to blame Hizbollah for starting the war and ultimately isolate the guerrillas politically. The strategy backfired, as Lebanese from all backgrounds cheered Hizbollah for beating back Israeli attacks.

Richard Armitage, a Republican and former deputy secretary of state, said, "The only thing that the bombing has achieved so far is to unite the population against the Israelis."[21]

Israel admitted using phosphorous artillery shells, a weapon many experts consider illegal under international law.[22] The UN reported that in the final days of the war, the Israel Defense Forces fired as many as four million cluster bomblets into civilian areas of southern Lebanon, of which an estimated one million failed to explode.[23]

The Israelis used American-made cluster bombs, which are less likely to detonate and therefore pose a greater threat to civilians. From the end of the war until the end of January 2007, 30 Lebanese civilians had died from these cluster bombs and another 180 had been injured.[24] U.S. law prohibits other countries from using American cluster bombs in civilian areas, but it appeared unlikely the Bush Administration would sanction Israel for its violations. For years to come, children and other civilians who stumble on the bomblets face maiming or death.

Jan Egeland, the UN's under secretary for humanitarian affairs, noted, "What's shocking—and I would say to me completely immoral—is that 90 percent of the cluster bomb strikes occurred in the last 72 hours of the conflict, when we knew there would be a resolution. Every day people are maimed, wounded and are killed by these ordnance."[25] Why would Israel fire cluster bombs when it had already agreed to a cease-fire? Israel wanted to make parts of Lebanon uninhabitable in order to weaken Hizbollah's political support.

Hizbollah also engaged in illegal activities by intentionally targeting civilians. Human Rights Watch reported that Hizbollah fired 113 rockets with about 4,400 cluster bomblets into northern Israel.[26] Human Rights Watch accused Hizbollah of war crimes for firing rockets indiscriminately into Israel, which killed both Israeli and Arab residents. In its report, Human Rights Watch wrote, "International humanitarian law (the laws of war) obliges warring parties to distinguish between combatants and civilians and, when attacking legitimate military targets, to ensure that the military advantage gained in the attack outweighs any possible harm caused to civilians."[27]

But the atrocities committed by both sides were hardly

equal. According to official Israeli figures, 120 IDF soldiers and 39 Israeli civilians died because of the fighting.[28] Experts have a harder time compiling accurate figures for Lebanon. The Higher Relief Commission, a Lebanese government agency, estimates the overall death toll at 1,181, including 34 Lebanese soldiers.[29] Hizbollah says 68 of its guerrillas died. Using those figures, Hizbollah killed roughly 3 Israeli soldiers for every civilian. The IDF killed roughly 17 Lebanese civilians for every combatant.

Israel claims that it killed about five hundred Hizbollah fighters, a figure that hasn't been corroborated elsewhere. But even assuming that figure is accurate, Israel still killed more than two civilians for every combatant.

Hizbollah clearly won the war politically. Opinion polls conducted immediately after the war showed 80 percent popular support for Hizbollah inside Lebanon, including backing from Sunni Muslims and Christians. In contrast, Israeli politicians and generals immediately began squabbling, blaming each other for the failure to decisively defeat Hizbollah. Prime Minister Olmert's popularity ratings sank below 40 percent among Israelis.

Even some staunch defenders of Tel Aviv admitted Israel lost. Former CIA analyst Kenneth Pollack noted, "Hizbollah did what no Arab government ever has: They fought Israel and didn't lose."[30]

So the war that was to strengthen the United States and Israel in the entire region resulted in a huge setback for both. Combined with the looming defeat of the United States in Iraq, the impact of the Israel-Lebanon War on Middle East relations will reverberate for years to come.

But to fully understand U.S. policy in the region, we must understand more about its recent history. For many Americans, U.S.-Iranian relations begin with the seizure of the U.S. Embassy in 1979. But for Iranians, the history goes back twenty-six years earlier.

FOUR

A Brief History
of U.S.-Iranian Relations

November 4, 1979, has gone down in history. That day, a group of militant, Islamic students took over the U.S. Embassy in Tehran. Although they didn't know it at the time, they helped alter U.S.-Iranian relations for decades.

The United States had backed the dictatorial shah for twenty-six years, and then after his overthrow, President Jimmy Carter allowed the shah to enter the United States for medical treatment. Iranians feared the United States was planning to return the shah to power as it had done in 1953.

At the time, I guessed the embassy takeover might last a few days or even a few weeks. I thought the hostages would be released, and Iranians could get on with sorting out their revolution. That was not to be. The crisis lasted 444 days. Ayatollah Ruhollah Khomeini used the mass anti-imperialist sentiment stirred up by the takeover to consolidate his power and wipe out opposition groups. That part is well known. What's not known, or often forgotten, is that inside the United States, we saw a huge rise in racism and xenophobia against Middle Easterners.

Some of my Iranian friends were attacked on the streets of
San Francisco for simply being Iranian. Similar incidents took
place around the country. Some Americans saw images of
American diplomats blindfolded and paraded on TV, and retaliated against any dark-skinned foreigner they could find.

The embassy takeover became a metaphor for U.S.-Iranian
relations. For people in the United States, it demonstrated international humiliation and the pure evil of a fundamentalist
regime intent on harming Americans. For Iranians, it showed
that the USA was trying to abort a popular revolution. Those
two sharply different perceptions of reality continue today.

It's All about Oil (and Geopolitics)

Iran has never been a formal colony, but the British exercised
virtual colonial control over Iran starting in the 1900s. In
1919, the British imposed the Anglo-Persian agreement on
Iran. British troops made sure that a British oil company controlled the country's oil production and export. The British
imposed martial law and ran the country's army, treasury, and
transport system.

British Foreign Secretary Lord George Curzon explained why
Iran was so important to the British Empire. He asked rhetori-
cally why Persia, as the country was then called, shouldn't rule
itself. "The answer is that her geographical position . . . renders
it impossible . . . . Further if Persia were to be alone, there is
every reason to fear that she would be overrun by Bolshevik influence from the north. Lastly, we possess . . . great assets in the
shape of oil fields, which are worked for the British navy and
which give us a commanding interest in that part of the world."[1]

That argument, with a few variations, has been used by

British and American governments ever since. Iran is blessed and cursed with a critical geographic location along shipping lanes of the Persian Gulf. Apparently, Iranians are not capable of handling those blessings without outside assistance.

The British remained the dominant power in Iran between the world wars. But the country emerged in turmoil by the end of World War II. As part of the wartime alliance, Soviet troops occupied northern Iran and British troops controlled the south. The British had forced Shah Reza Pahlavi to abdicate in 1941 and crowned his son Mohammad Reza Pahlavi as king, but the young shah was inexperienced and weak. Both Kurds and Azerbaijanis briefly established leftist, independent states, and the Tudeh (communist) Party was growing in strength.

Iran was supposed to be a constitutional monarchy with both a king and a parliament. But for most of the 1900s, the British and the shah made sure the parliament played a subservient role or no role at all. But Iran, like many countries in the developing world, was no longer willing to settle for the old power structure and traditional subservience to colonial powers. Starting in 1944, Shah Mohammad Reza Pahlavi lost power to the elected parliament.

The recently invigorated parliamentary opposition was led by Mohammad Mossadegh, a wealthy and aristocratic nationalist who had been active in Iranian politics for thirty years. He strongly believed in western-style democracy, a free press, multi-party politics, and an independent judiciary— what today we would call civil society. He also strongly opposed British domination of Iran.

Mossadegh led the National Front, which was allied with a variety of religious, nationalist, socialist, and communist groups. Mossadegh supported what leftists called a united front. Each party figured it would benefit from the alliance and opening up of democracy while maintaining its own views on the best long-term solutions for Iran. The United States vilified such coalitions because, supposedly, Moscow-controlled communists used them to sneak into power. In reality, the United States wanted everyone to support it against the USSR and to allow Western companies to pump Iran's oil.

Mansour Farhang, a former Iranian ambassador to the United States who later taught at Bennington College, said U.S. officials "didn't believe in neutrality, they didn't believe in authentic democratic development within a country that was not an ally of the West or the East."[2]

The Oily British

The stakes were high in Iran. A corrupt shah in 1901 had sold a British financier exclusive rights to develop oil and gas in Iran for sixty years. The British government later bought part of the financier's stake and became 50 percent owner of Anglo-Iranian Oil. Under tremendous Iranian pressure in 1933, Britain modified the agreement to give more money to Iran but also expanded the exclusive contract until 1993. While Iran was supposed to share in the profits, in practice Anglo-Iranian made out like the robber barons of old. In 1947, Anglo-Iranian reported profits of $112 million, but only $19.6 million went to the Iranian government.[3]

The Majlis (parliament) demanded that the British share 50 percent of their profits and open their books to Iranian auditors. American oil companies had set up a 50 percent ownership deal with Saudi Arabia's government in 1950, so Iran's proposal was quite reasonable. But Anglo-Iranian Oil and the British government refused and insisted on the terms of the old contract. The crisis led directly to the Majlis' electing Mossadegh prime minister by an overwhelming 79-to-12 vote in April 1950. The Majlis then voted, in principle, to nationalize British oil interests altogether.

Remember, this was still the colonial era, in which the British Empire stretched across the globe. The British officials took the Majlis vote as a challenge to their colonial hegemony and immediately conspired to get rid of the democratic government.

In May 1951 the Majlis formally established a state-run oil company. The British refused to cooperate with the new company and later withdrew managers and skilled personnel. The huge Abadan oil refinery in southern Iran eventually ground to a halt. British tankers refused to export Iran's crude oil. The British navy established an illegal sea blockade of Iran's ports and stopped any other country from transporting the oil. Britain acted unilaterally, without a UN vote. The International Court of Justice at The Hague eventually ruled against Britain and Anglo-Iranian Oil, but that didn't stop Britain from continued illegal military activity.

While Iran began to suffer economically from the oil embargo, Mossadegh remained tremendously popular. So Britain tried to convince President Harry Truman to support a coup. Truman refused and suggested that Britain reach a compromise with Iran.

Mossadegh became a hero worldwide. Iran's defiance of British imperialism became a popular cause in Asia, Africa, and Latin America. Many in the United States sympathized with Iran as well. Mossadegh came to New York to speak before the UN and received a warm welcome. *Time* magazine named him Man of the Year in 1951, calling him the "Iranian George Washington."

Then Dwight Eisenhower got elected. Even before the new president took office in January 1953, his top advisors were planning to support a coup in Iran. The British, who were fighting to maintain their oil monopoly, argued that the Soviet Union might take over Iran because of Mossadegh's weak control of the government. That was the argument that won over the Eisenhower Administration.[4]

The CIA dispatched Kermit Roosevelt, Jr., grandson of President Teddy Roosevelt, to Tehran, where he set about conniving, lying, and bribing anyone available. British spies turned over their agents to the CIA, who promptly put them and various members of the Majlis on the CIA payroll. The CIA secretly shipped Roosevelt over $1 million in cash, a considerable sum in those days.

The United States sought to erode Mossadegh's majority in the Majlis, as well as win over police and military officials. But underhanded political deals and bribery proved insufficient. So the CIA turned to violence.

Terrorism, the Clergy, and the Coup

On April 19, 1953, Iranians on the CIA payroll kidnapped the pro-Mossadegh Tehran police chief, General Mahmoud Afshartus. They held him in a cave outside of Tehran. As police came to his rescue, a captor shot him. Of course, the United States kept its role in the kidnapping secret. Stephen Kinzer wrote in his excellent book *All the Shah's Men*, "The murder had the desired effect. It shocked the country and also eliminated a popular officer who might have been a formidable obstacle to the success of the forthcoming coup."[5]

Some major Muslim clergy had initially supported Mossadegh and opposed the British. The CIA worked hard to break that alliance. As explained in a declassified CIA report on the coup, CIA agents issued "black propaganda in the name of the Tudeh Party, threatening these [religious] leaders with savage punishment if they opposed Mossadeq. Threatening phone calls were also made to them, in the name of Tudeh, and one of several planned sham bombings of the houses of these leaders was carried out."[6]

Similarly, the CIA had agent provocateurs organize phony Tudeh demonstrations that ransacked the offices of another political party, thus driving a wedge between the two.[7]

Ayatollah Abulqasim Kashani was a fundamentalist Shiite mullah very much admired by today's clerical leaders. He had fought in the desert against the British, been imprisoned, and then been exiled by the shah. He was elected to the Majlis while exiled in Beirut. Popular support forced the shah to allow his return. Kashani initially supported Mossadegh and his decision to nationalize the country's oil.

But CIA-allied politicians managed to alienate Kashani from Mossadegh and eventually involve him in the coup plot. Roosevelt sent Kashani $10,000 the day before the coup, and Kashani helped mobilize pro-shah demonstrators at a crucial moment.[8] Kashani showed up at the airport to welcome the shah's return to Tehran and was personally greeted by him.[9]

The U.S. Propaganda

Most mainstream American newspapers, magazines, and radio broadcasts of the time reflected the official U.S. propaganda line that Iran had gone though a popular uprising against an unstable and communist-leaning Mossadegh. Universal Newsreel releases distributed to movie theaters nationwide every week were typical: "In the quick shift of power, Mossadegh was finally apprehended and held for treason. The shah, who had fled to Rome, comes home, backed by General Zahedi, military strongman who engineered his return to power. . . . Iranian oil may again flow—westward!" The Newsreel segment ends with a mighty musical flourish.[10]

In fact, American historians now admit to what Iranians have known since 1953: the CIA and British engineered a coup against a democratic government in order to install a pro-Western, anti-communist regime. Mark Gasiorowski, a political science professor at Louisiana State University and expert on the coup, wrote, "The CIA extensively stage-managed the entire coup, not only carrying it out but also preparing the groundwork for it by subordinating various important Iranian political actors and using propaganda and other instruments to influence public opinion against Mossadeq. . . . In my view, this thoroughly refutes the argument that is commonly made in Iranian monarchist exile circles that the coup was a legitimate 'popular uprising' on behalf of the shah."[11]

After the coup, the shah turned over most of the country's oil production to foreign firms. U.S. oil companies ended up taking a 50 percent share of Iranian oil production while Anglo-Iranian Oil got only 40 percent.[12] Ironically, Britain would have come out ahead if it had accepted Iran's earlier offer of half ownership. But the American victory in the 1953 coup was just one indication that the British Empire was in decline.

The Shah Gets a Makeover

When the coup initially met setbacks, Shah Mohammad Reza Pahlavi fled to Baghdad and then Rome. When the coup proved successful, he returned to Tehran to serve as figurehead for the United States. His military and police cracked down hard on the democratic forces, jailing opponents, closing newspapers, and banning political parties. The U.S. government, the great promoter of democracy, had crushed it in Iran. But, of course, that's not what U.S. officials said publicly.

The U.S. government, echoed by the media, praised the shah as a modernizer who saved his country from chaos and doom. Soon after the coup, the shah visited New York and met with Mayor Robert Wagner, Jr. In a broadcast of that visit on WNYC public radio, the announcer intoned, "The shah has always had one thing uppermost in mind to improve the lot of his people. . . . The shah's well-rounded personality is felt throughout Iran and has resulted in the balanced manner in which he has handled crises in Iran."

The Capitulation

The United States established close military ties with the shah. And that led to a major dispute regarding the legal status of U.S. military personnel. The United States had stationed soldiers in Iran since 1947 to train local armed forces and police. By the end of the shah's rule, the United States had 185 military trainers in Iran, the largest U.S. mission in any third world country at the time.[13]

Then, as now, the United States insisted that its military personnel not be subject to other countries' civil or criminal courts. The United States argues that local judicial systems cannot fairly judge U.S. military personnel, or even their family members. So the United States coerces other countries to sign treaties that stipulate Americans can be tried only by American courts. Few Americans give this system of extraterritoriality a second thought. But in many parts of the world, it's a major flash point. The shah's signing of such a treaty in 1964 is known to Iranians as "the capitulation."

Ayatollah Khomeini rose to national prominence because of his outspoken opposition to the capitulation. In October 1964 he criticized the United States and the shah. Stanford University Iran expert Professor Abbas Milani said Khomeini used a famous example. "If an American sergeant kills the shah of Iran, we can't take him to court. But if the shah of Iran does the slightest thing to an American, they will take him out." Milani said, "Before that [speech] Khomeini was a secondhand cleric," but after his criticism, he became known throughout Iran.[14]

In direct response to that criticism of the capitulation, the shah exiled Khomeini in November 1964. Khomeini went first to Turkey then later to Najaf, Iraq. Khomeini continued to agitate against the shah and gained considerable popularity. By the late 1970s, Iran was ready to explode.

The 1979 Revolution and Embassy Takeover

By 1978 the shah's power had begun to fade. Students, workers, women, and the religious community were fed up. But the United States, always focused on the supposed communist threat, was largely unaware of the ferment among Iranian Muslims. In January 1978, religion students in the holy city of Qom demonstrated, demanding that Ayatollah Khomeini be allowed to return from exile. Police opened fire and killed seventy students.

Shiites traditionally commemorate martyrs forty days after their deaths. So forty days later, Iranians demonstrated in Tabriz, and police killed over a hundred. The demonstrations and repression escalated until the infamous "Black Friday," September 8, when the foreign media reported that forces loyal to the shah murdered several hundred in Tehran, although some historians put the number at less than a hundred.[15]

By October, workers had gone on strike, including oil workers. The shah declared martial law, but strikes and massive demonstrations continued. On January 16, 1979, the shah fled for his life. By mid-February Ayatollah Khomeini had returned to declare the Islamic Republic.

Khomeini initially enjoyed support from all the non-monarchist groupings in Iran. He appointed Mehdi Bazargan, a cabinet minister under Mossadegh, as prime minister. Bazargan appointed a cabinet made up mostly of nationalists, with clerics assigned to sub-cabinet-level posts. Political parties operated freely; newspapers of various stripes published and circulated widely. But all that changed very rapidly by the fall of 1979.

In October 1979 the shah entered the United States for cancer treatment. We now know that the shah was indeed seriously ill with cancer, but at the time, many Iranians suspected a trick. Militant students knew that Iranian government officials had met with President Jimmy Carter's representatives and feared Iran would normalize relations with the United States.

On November 4, militant students marched up to the U.S. Embassy in Tehran, a block-long fortress with concrete walls. They pushed past the Marine guards and occupied the building. They tied up the embassy staff and demanded that the United States return the shah to Iran for trial and punishment. The students captured a total of sixty-six hostages that day, but released some women and African Americans over the next few weeks. Ultimately, fifty-two diplomatic personnel were held at the embassy.

Massoumeh Ebtekar, press spokesperson for the students, then known as Tehran Mary, explained the widely different perceptions of Americans and Iranians at the time. She had become vice president in charge of the environment ministry when I interviewed her in 2000.

"America had lost a lot," she told me. "They had lost an ally. They had lost what they called the gendarme of the region. So something serious was going on." Ebtekar said the students knew the history of the CIA coup against Mossadegh. "Many people felt that history was being repeated."[16] She said the students originally planned to stay a few hours at the embassy to make their point. But the situation shifted rapidly.

The student takeover crystallized anti-imperialist sentiment among Iranians and became incredibly popular. After years of coups, repression by the shah, extraterritoriality, and other indignities, Iranians saw someone standing up to the United States. The U.S. government spread a lot of disinformation in those days, claiming the occupiers weren't really students acting independently.

The people inside the embassy were indeed students drawn from several Tehran universities. They had acted without the advance knowledge of Khomeini or the Iranian government. Prime Minister Bazargan and his cabinet, however, realized the seriousness of the crisis. The students had seized a diplomatic compound, which is legally U.S. territory, and the resulting publicity had blackened the eye of the Iranian government. Bazargan and his cabinet, realizing that their power was on the wane, resigned en masse one day after the student takeover.

Khomeini backed the students and their demands. As a result the standoff went from a few hours to weeks, and ultimately to 444 days.

Barry Rosen, press spokesman for the embassy in 1979, told me in a 2000 interview that the first few weeks of captivity were horrendous.

> We were tied hand and foot. They would take some of the cord from the drapes and tie you up. I was forced to sleep bound hand and foot for several days. They were so frightened of us. They thought we were all members of the CIA. They had seen many motion pictures of James Bond over the years. They were frightened and thought that we were supermen. There were moments when the Iranians interrogated us. There were times when they put guns to our heads and counted from ten to one and said answer or we'll shoot you. [17]

Rosen said that physical conditions got better after a few weeks. But the hostages still had to endure mental anguish, sometimes held in dank cellars and prisons. Even twenty years later, however, Ebtekar doesn't apologize for that treatment.

"It's a matter of collective rights [versus] individual rights," she said. "It is very difficult to compare the sufferings that the Iranian nation felt during fifty years of foreign domination and comparing that to the sufferings or the pain they may have faced during these 444 days." [18]

The Revolution Goes Sour

While many of the former leaders of the embassy takeover won't apologize for their actions, they do admit that reactionary forces within the clerical elite used the event to consolidate power. A number of former captors, including Ebtekar and Abbas Abdi, became leading advocates of political reform.

Many of the former student leaders want a democratic, Islamic government. Ebtekar told me the former students have become part of "a reform movement that genuinely believes that Islam and democracy can go along with each other, believes in the freedom of expression, believes in the fact that an Islamic society can tolerate . . . a wide spectrum of different viewpoints and different interpretations."

Abdi told me his ideas about the revolution have matured. "At the time of the shah, our picture of a democratic system was not a very realistic one. Obviously people who live under a despotic regime may aspire and wish for a democratic regime, but the image that they have may be a variation of that same despotic regime."[19]

In 1997 Abdi flew to Paris to meet with Barry Rosen.

In a sense, Rosen had exchanged roles with his former captors. He no longer felt the pressure of being an embassy spokesperson. But Abdi faced tremendous responsibilities as a prominent political reformer who had been jailed several times for his outspoken views. Rosen told me about his thoughts before the meeting.

"I didn't know if I could forgive," he said. "I don't forget what went on. I will never forget that. As soon as we met, we started to talk. It's as if everything melted away. We still had different points of view. Abbas Abdi is now a man who is fighting for some law and order in Iran, to build a democratic system within the country."

Rosen and Abdi reconciled themselves on a personal level. But the rendezvous did nothing to warm up relations between the U.S. and Iranian governments. Abdi later published the results of a survey indicating 70 percent of Iranians wanted a political reconciliation with the United States, for which he was arrested and served three years in jail.

Ironically, the people that Americans most hated are now the ones who want to reach out to the United States.

Never Negotiate with Terrorists?

Back in 1979, President Carter knew his presidency was on the line when the hostage crisis continued to drag on, month after month. The ABC news program *Nightline* began as a series of specials covering the hostage crisis. Each night, host Ted Koppel prominently displayed the number of days the hostages had been held. Carter adopted increasingly belligerent and aggressive policies.

Carter initially cut off diplomatic relations and seized $8 billion in Iranian assets, including airplanes and other equipment already paid for. The United States imposed a trade embargo and cut off all Iranian oil imports. In April 1980, the United States attempted a clandestine military mission to rescue the hostages, called Operation Eagle Claw. It was a disaster. A sandstorm caused so much confusion at a rendezvous point fifty miles outside Tehran that the mission was aborted. Then a U.S. helicopter collided with a C130 cargo plane, killing eight soldiers. That sealed the fate of the hostages and Carter himself, who lost to Ronald Reagan in the 1980 election.

The public didn't know at the time, but Reagan emissaries met secretly with Iranian officials to arrange release of embassy hostages after the election.[20] Under terms of the hostage release formally negotiated by the Carter Admin-

istration, the United States signed the Algiers Agreement.
The United States returned some of Iran's impounded money,
gave Iran immunity from lawsuits, and pledged not to inter-
vene politically or militarily in Iran's internal affairs.[21] The
hostages were put on airplanes and left Iranian airspace just
minutes after Reagan formally took office on January 20,
1981. And this came courtesy of politicians who say "never
negotiate with terrorists."

The Iran-Contra Affair

In August 1985, Israeli intelligence officials approached the
Reagan Administration with an unlikely proposal: Israel
wanted to help arm Iran.[22] At first such a proposal would
seem strange. After all, Iran stood as a sworn enemy of the
"Zionist entity." But Israel at the time saw Iraq as a greater
danger, and it therefore tilted toward Iran in its war with Iraq.

The Reagan Administration also liked the plan because in
return for arms, the Iranians promised to free American
hostages held in Lebanon. The deal was done.

In August 1985, Israel provided one hundred antiaircraft
missiles to Iran as a first installment. Both the United States
and Israel would supply tens of millions of dollars in aircraft
spare parts, ammunition, and armaments to Iran. Iran paid
the United States for the arms, and then the Reagan Administration secretly used the money to arm the Contras fighting
the leftist government of Nicaragua.

The Reagan Administration violated all kinds of laws with
this scheme, from failing to notify Congress of covert operations, to arming the Contras in direct violation of the Boland
Amendment passed by Congress. A few Reagan officials were
prosecuted for minor aspects of the scandal. The main perpe-

trators, including Lieutenant Colonel Oliver North, got off. Reagan himself never faced impeachment.

While Iran-Contra has gone down in American history as a horrible scandal, it's rarely mentioned in Iran. The Iranian government was pleased to receive much-needed arms. Iranian officials I interviewed admitted that Iran accepted help from Israel, but they dismissed cooperation as a wartime necessity.

The USS *Vincennes* Incident

I still remember the day that the USS *Vincennes* shot down Iranian Air flight 655 on July 3, 1988. I was teaching journalism at California State University, Hayward (now East Bay), when initial news reports indicated the USS *Vincennes* had fired in self-defense to stop an attack by an Iranian aircraft.[23] I told my students that something was very wrong with this story and to watch it closely in the days ahead.

It made no sense for an Iranian plane to attack the far-superior U.S. Navy, then stationed in the Persian Gulf. If something makes no sense politically, then it probably makes no sense militarily. I told my students about the 1964 Gulf of Tonkin incident, in which North Vietnamese naval vessels allegedly attacked U.S. ships on the high seas. The Lyndon Johnson Administration used the attack-that-never-happened to justify the Vietnam War.

I didn't think the *Vincennes* incident was a prelude to war, but I suspected the United States was engaging in the same kind of confabulation. The United States quickly admitted that it had shot down a civilian airliner but tried to blame the Iranians for the incident. Ronald Reagan issued a statement on July 3 that read, in part, "The course of the Iranian civilian airliner was such that it was headed directly for the USS *Vin-*

cennes . . . . When the aircraft failed to heed repeated warnings, the *Vincennes* followed standing orders and widely publicized procedures, firing to protect itself against possible attack."[24]

The administration later claimed that Iran Air flight 655 failed to turn on its transponder identifying itself as a civilian plane, was flying outside the proper civilian air corridor, and was rapidly descending toward the USS *Vincennes*, then sailing in international waters. The Reagan Administration said that while the United States regretted the tragic loss of life, the U.S. Navy did nothing wrong.

None of the administration's key assertions turned out to be true. The USS *Vincennes* was illegally inside Iranian waters. It wasn't under attack. Iran Air flight 655 was within the corridor for civilian flights and was ascending, not descending. In short, the United States had shot down a civilian airliner doing nothing out of the ordinary.[25]

The Iranian government argued that the United States intentionally shot down the aircraft as part of an effort to assist Saddam Hussein in Iraq's war with Iran. In April 1988, the United States had engaged in a naval battle with Iran. U.S. ships severely damaged two large Iranian vessels and six armed speedboats in what was called Operation Praying Mantis. So the Iranians concluded that the shooting down of Iran Air flight 655 constituted a warning of all-out war.

But numerous independent investigations have never shown the shooting was intentional. If the United States was trying to send a message to Iran, it could have done so through additional attacks on military targets, as occurred in Operation Praying Mantis. Intentionally shooting down a civilian airliner made sense neither politically nor from a public relations standpoint.

It seems likely that aggressive Navy officers, operating under orders to engage Iranian ships if necessary, erroneously identified Iran Air flight 655 as a hostile aircraft. When the enormity of the mistake became apparent, the Navy covered up the crime.

A 1992 *Newsweek* magazine investigative report explained, "The top Pentagon brass understood from the beginning that if the whole truth about the *Vincennes* came out, it would mean months of humiliating headlines. So the U.S. Navy did what all navies do after terrible blunders at sea: it told lies and handed out medals."[26]

The United States did eventually pay $61.8 *million* in compensation to victims' families but never admitted fault. By comparison, Libya had to pay $2.7 *billion* for its role in the 1988 explosion of the Pan American flight downed over Lockerbie, Scotland. And in perhaps the greatest insult, the crew of the *Vincennes* all got combat ribbons. Lieutenant Commander Scott Lustig, air war coordinator on the *Vincennes*, received the Commendation Medal for "heroic achievement."

The Iran Air flight 655 tragedy is permanently seared in the collective Iranian memory. Two hundred ninety people, including sixty-six children, lost their lives for no reason. What if Iran accidentally shot down a United Airlines passenger plane? The U.S. government might use that as an excuse to wage war. But somehow it's different when innocent Iranians die.

Support for Terrorism?

Over the years the United States has accused Iran of being the most active state sponsor of terrorism in the world. But that description conflates real incidents of terrorism with armed actions most of the world considers fighting for national liberation.

Iranian Revolutionary Guards helped found the Lebanese group Hizbollah, for example. Iran helps arm Hizbollah, which has killed innocent Israeli civilians. Hizbollah was also responsible for driving a truck bomb into the U.S. Marine base in Lebanon in 1983, killing 241 service personnel. But that was an armed action intended to drive foreign troops out of their country. If Hizbollah had an air force, it would have dropped bombs on the barracks.

These days Hizbollah is both a guerrilla group and a political party with considerable power in the Lebanese parliament. The United States calls Hizbollah "terrorist" as a means to attack a political group that has effectively stymied U.S. plans in Lebanon.

Similarly, Iran gives political and military backing to the Palestinian group Hamas. Hamas has taken credit for numerous suicide bombings inside Israel that have killed and wounded hundreds of innocent civilians. Hamas also won a plurality of the popular vote in the January 2006 Palestinian Authority election and 56 percent of the parliamentary seats. It provides social services for hundreds of thousands of Palestinians. Hamas is both a political and a military movement. Simply denouncing Hamas as terrorists, while blaming Iran for supporting them, doesn't help resolve the underlying question of Palestinian nationhood.

I strongly oppose the political ideology of both Hizbollah and Hamas, which is based on a fundamentalist interpretation of Islam. There is no excuse for terror tactics that kill innocent civilians. But for years, the United States has funded and supported precisely such terror tactics by groups and governments that it supports.[27] The people of Lebanon and Palestine can determine what to do about Hizbollah and Hamas, and they will ultimately force those groups to move away from terrorist tactics.

The United States has also accused Iran of organizing terrorist attacks such as the 1994 bombing of a Jewish community center in Argentina. Evidence of who was behind that bombing remains murky. Authorities in Argentina say Iran is responsible, but Iran denies responsibility. Similarly, the United States accuses Iran of organizing the attack on the Khobar Towers housing complex in Saudi Arabia. The 1996 truck bomb attack killed 19 American military personnel and wounded 372 Americans and Saudis. Iran denies responsibility, and some sources blamed Al Qaeda for the attack.[28]

Iranian intelligence agents *were* responsible, however, for the assassinations of Iranian and Kurdish opposition leaders living in Europe, based on police investigations in those countries.[29] In the 1990s, Iranian intelligence services were also responsible for carrying out terrorist assassinations of writers and opposition figures inside Iran.

Gary Sick, a senior research scholar at Columbia University's School of International and Public Affairs, noted that Iran has not been sponsoring terrorist groups outside the Middle East in recent years. He wrote, "Today, Iran's promotion of violence seems to be increasingly focused on support for radical anti-Israeli groups. . . . This shift calls for a different and more creative set of responses on the part of the United States."[30]

Some Recent History

In general, U.S.-Iranian relations have remained mutually hostile in recent years. The September 11, 2001 terrorist attacks on the United States briefly changed that. The Iranian government cooperated with the United States in its efforts to overthrow the Taliban in Afghanistan. This may come as a surprise to those who think of Islamic fundamentalists as all in cahoots, but Iran solidly opposed Taliban rule. The Taliban murdered nine Iranian diplomats in 1998, almost leading the two countries to war.[31] Iran had supported the Northern Alliance fighting the Taliban.

So when the United States was planning to invade Afghanistan, Iran was happy to help. Iran assisted in forging a coalition of Afghan opposition forces at the Bonn conference that established an interim Afghan government. U.S. officials praised Iran's "constructive role" in the meetings.[32] In January 2002, Iran pledged $560 million for Afghan reconstruction aid, the largest amount offered from a third world country.[33] Iranian officials have told me that they expected the United States to extend the contacts over Afghanistan into a wider dialogue about U.S.-Iranian relations.

Instead, in his State of the Union address in January 2002, President Bush denounced Iran as part of an "axis of evil." The Bush Administration closed off any possibility of reaching a political settlement with Iran and began its campaign for regime change. The Bush Administration regularly reminds Iran that "all options remain on the table," including possible military attacks.

But as the administration soon discovered, it's a lot easier to talk about regime change than to do it. That's because, among other problems, the United States really doesn't understand who rules Iran.

FIVE

Who Rules Iran?

Two impeccably dressed men approached us at a trendy north Tehran espresso bar in 2005. They wanted to know if Sean Penn would like to interview Akbar Hashemi Rafsanjani, then the leading candidate for president. Rafsanjani is known in Iran as "Akbar Shah" (the great king) and is reputedly one of the wealthiest men in the country. He wasn't giving many interviews to the foreign media at the time, so we accepted, figuring nothing would likely happen. But, to our surprise, the interview did eventually take place. We were about to begin a strange and convoluted journey that revealed a lot about how the power structure works in Iran today.

In his five-part series for the *San Francisco Chronicle*, Sean referred to the pin-stripped guys at the cafe as "the Siths," the evil characters in the final *Star Wars* saga.[1] At the time, we just called them "the Chanels" because one of the guys handed me a business card indicating he ran a boutique selling Chanel perfumes.

Mr. Chanel assured us that he was very close friends with

top Rafsanjani advisors. He could get us the interview, really. And by the way, would Sean like to come to dinner at his house? As strange as this may seem to non-Iranians, we must have received thirty unsolicited dinner invitations during Sean's few days in Tehran. Iranians are incredibly hospitable, and people were quite serious about the offer. (I'm not sure what would have happened if we had actually accepted any of the offers, often made by complete strangers on the street. Husband to wife: "Hi, Honey, I'm home, and I brought Sean Penn. Can you throw a few kebabs on the fire?")

We declined Chanel's invitation to dinner. That night Chanel called and said we should meet him at 10:30 p.m. Right—we go meet some stranger, in some strange location, in a strange city in the middle of the night. We politely declined again.

But over the next few days, we found out that the Chanels were real. The first Chanel had a friend, who had a friend, who was related to a guy who really was a top Rafsanjani advisor. That's how a lot of business and political deals get made in Iran. Economic wealth overlaps with family, political, and religious connections. In the shah's time, people said Iran was run by one thousand families. That's still true, but the families have changed. For example, Iran's nuclear negotiator Ali Larajani's father is the well-known Ayatollah Mirza Hashem Amoli.[2] Reformist leader Mohammad Reza Khatami, brother of the former president, is married to the granddaughter of Ayatollah Khomeini.[3] And former president Khatami is the son of a grand ayatollah.

The next afternoon we met at a north Tehran rendezvous point and a multicar convoy chugged up a winding road. We were on a private, military-patrolled street leading to the for-

mer home of Ayatollah Khomeini in the Jamaran neighborhood, less than a mile from the shah's old Niavaran Palace.

But Khomeini had been an ascetic from the old school, es-
chewing ostentatious wealth. A guide taking us around the
compound stressed that back in 1979 Khomeini had stopped
his supporters from an elaborate remodeling of the building.
The Ayatollah, we were told, preferred simple rugs, a few
chairs, and tables. But that asceticism didn't transfer to
Khomeini's allies, who stayed in power over the next twenty-
eight years.

On the way up the private road, we passed by Rafsanjani's
enormous compound, protected by a large metal fence. Not
bad digs for a man who began life as the son of small-scale
pistachio farmers. Technically, the government owns the
houses, not the individuals. But the opulence belies the myth
of humble religious people living the ascetic life.

Corruption is rampant among top political and business
leaders. Iran ranks 2.7 on Transparency International's 2006
Corruption Perceptions Index, with 1 being the most corrupt
and 10 being the most honest.[4] It ranked 106th in the world,
behind such countries as Mongolia and Mozambique. Under
the shah's rule, a small group of corrupt officials became fabulously wealthy. Under clerical rule, the corruption remains—
it's just covered by turbans.

Iran's Political System

Iran's political system is unique in the world. Iran is neither
a secular state nor a theocracy, neither a totalitarian dictatorship nor a representative democracy. Conservative religious,
military, and business leaders have institutional control over

major government decisions, but they are constrained by
elections and sometimes raucous political debate.

Let me make an analogy to the U.S. political system.
Imagine that a popular uprising brings a Christian fundamentalist to power. He declares himself the Supreme Christian
Leader, and his religious supporters write a new constitution
in which the United States becomes a "Christian Republic."
Then the Supreme Christian Leader holds a referendum on
the new constitution, and it passes overwhelmingly.

The Supreme Christian Leader appoints Pat Robertson and
other Christian elders to the Supreme Court. All members of
the Senate, who are popularly elected, are evangelical Christian ministers; even Catholic priests can't get elected. The
Congress is still elected in competitive elections. The Congress even sets aside a certain number of seats for Jews, Muslims, and other non-Christians. But the Senate decides who
meets "Christian qualifications" to run for any political office
and can even disqualify sitting members of Congress from
seeking reelection. The Supreme Christian Leader can inter-
vene at any time in any of the political institutions, and his
word comes from God.

That's Iran, only they're not Christian.

So Iran certainly isn't democratic. But Iran is far more
responsive to the popular will than governments in such
American-allied countries as Saudi Arabia or Kuwait, which
are dictatorial monarchies, and where women as well as
ethnic/religious minorities have no rights. The Iranian government has held more than twenty-two elections in which
competing conservative factions and the loyal opposition
camps debated issues and vied for support. But when the
democratic process challenges the power of the religious and

economic elite, the religious and repressive institutions hold sway.[5] So it's critical to understand both the economic and political power of Iran's ruling elite.

Iran's economy has been called Islamic socialism because so many key industries are nationalized. But clerical capitalism would be a better description. Iran has a free enterprise system with government and quasi-governmental institutions monopolizing large sectors of the economy. Large private businesses exist, and some of their owners wield considerable political power. The economy does little to benefit ordinary Iranians, but it has created a fabulously wealthy new ruling class.

Let's take a look at some of the competing interest groups.

The Bazaar Merchants

After descending into the labyrinth of Tehran's covered bazaar, a visitor passes hundreds of small stands and shops selling everything from housewares to handwoven Persian carpets. Thousands of merchants buy, sell, and export products here six days a week. The store owners welcome you with a cup of tea and explain how they can make you a very special deal. They dress casually in slacks and white shirts with open collars. But some of these bazaar merchants (bazaaris) are quite wealthy and constitute a key economic sector in Iran's power structure.

Dating back before the 1979 revolution, some of the bazaaris had longtime ties to the local clergy and were marginalized by the shah. Many of the wealthy bazaaris felt threatened by such modern innovations as chain stores. The bazaaris see themselves as upholders of Islamic traditions.

Wealthy bazaaris provided the financial backbone for Ayatollah Khomeini in exile, supported his revolution, and became some of his strongest political supporters when he came
to power.

Some of the bazaaris went on to become leaders of the
Revolutionary Guard and the revolutionary foundations
(bonyads). Many of them continue to support conservative
candidates for parliament and other elected bodies, although
some supported the reformists. Conservative bazaaris control
the important chambers of commerce, and the ruling clergy
bestow valuable favors on them.

One bazaari living in Dubai wanted to export fifteen thousand pairs of shoes to Iran. But paying customs duties made
the transaction too costly, and smuggling them into Iran on
small boats was too risky. So he bribed a Revolutionary
Guard intelligence official to facilitate the deal. The shoes arrived in Tehran three days later, shipped by air.

The Bonyads—Revolutionary Foundations

The Islamic Republic set up a vast network of bonyads as a
way to help the poor, war veterans, and others. The government funded them by turning over property confiscated from
the shah and his wealthy supporters, who fled the country
after 1979. The bonyads, because they are considered nonprofit charities, can import luxury goods without paying
taxes. The bonyad leaders soon became a major economic
force outside the control of the parliament, president, central
bank, or anyone else except the Supreme Leader, who appoints them.

In 2006 Mohammed Forouzandeh, a former defense minister, headed the Foundation of the Oppressed and Disabled, the country's largest bonyad, made up of some four hundred firms. The government gave the foundation factories and other assets confiscated from the shah's supporters. It employs four hundred thousand workers and has assets of as much as $12 billion.[6] The bonyads run all kinds of businesses and account for an estimated 10 to 20 percent of Iran's gross domestic product.[7]

Because the bonyads operate outside normal government control and don't show their financial books to outsiders, corruption runs rampant. Morteza Rafiqdoost, brother of the former head of the Foundation of the Oppressed and Disabled and himself part of the bonyad, received a life sentence in the mid-1990s for stealing $400 million.[8]

The bonyads are a source of financing for conservative political movements. One bonyad, the Panzdah-e-Khordad, put up the $2.8 million bounty to kill British writer Salman Rushdie after Ayatollah Khomeini issued his infamous fatwa accusing the author of blasphemy.[9]

The Revolutionary Guard

After the 1979 revolution, the clerical leaders didn't trust the loyalty of the regular armed forces. So they formed the Islamic Revolutionary Guard Corps (IRGC) as a more reliable military organization. Its soldiers serve a variety of positions, including as a Praetorian guard to safeguard leaders and as border and security police.

Over the past twenty years, the IRGC have taken over more than a hundred economic enterprises to become financially self-sufficient and to avoid financial accountability through the regular government budgeting process.[10] The IRGC control ports and airports and have become a major factor in the construction industry. An IRGC subsidiary got part of the oil contract in the South Pars gas field and a $1.3 billion contract for a natural gas pipeline.[11] Its leading members have become extremely wealthy.[12]

Hooshang Amirahmadi, director of the Center for Middle Eastern Studies at Rutgers University, told me that the Revolutionary Guard uses political influence to bolster its economic power and corrupt practices, including the importation of smuggled goods such as liquor. "A lot of ministers and governors are from the Revolutionary Guard," he said. "They are using the money to buy loyalty and create power bases."[13]

The Revolutionary Guard shows no hesitancy in using that power. In 2005, the IRGC was discovered to be running an illegal airport near Karaj City, close to Tehran. They were able to import and export goods without any oversight. That same year, President Khatami attended a ceremony to open the new Imam Khomeini International Airport in Tehran. After the formalities, the Revolutionary Guard stormed the airport and shut it down. It later reopened, but under Revolutionary Guard management.[14]

The Government Bureaucrats

About 70 percent of the economy is state owned. Oil, autos, and petrochemicals and much of banking, shipping, transportation, communication, and import/export are under government control. So the Islamic Republic employs hundreds of thousands of people in state industries, including hundreds of top managers who have a vested interest in maintaining clerical capitalism. They are expected to throw their support behind the current ruling faction in government, and they can lose their jobs when another faction takes power.

Major Tehran hotels are owned by bonyads. For example, the former Intercontinental Hotel, now called the Laleh, is owned by one powerful bonyad. You can still see the Intercon logo on some of the dishes and old furniture. In 2005 I became acquainted with the manager, Mr. Alizadeh. He seemed like a nice enough guy, if a bit long-winded. We stayed in touch by e-mail. After the election of President Ahmadinejad, he stopped returning my e-mails. I later found out he was removed from his position soon after Ahmadinejad's inauguration. His departure was part of a more widespread purge of company managers and the diplomatic corps.

Alliances Form and Break Apart

There's a reason foreigners have a hard time figuring out what's going on in Iran. The ruling elite doesn't break down into easily defined categories, nor do political parties reflect strong ideological trends. The various power centers come together on some issues, only to break apart at a later time. Both Democratic and Republican leaders in the United States have been befuddled by the Iranian system.

In the 1980s, for example, the Reagan Administration said it was trying to promote Iranian moderates over the hardliners. Reagan officials held secret talks with supporters of President Rafsanjani, whom they thought of as a moderate and realist. During the Iran-Contra scandal, Reagan's boys—among them Lieutenant Colonel Oliver North and Donald Rumsfeld—secretly allowed Iran to obtain missiles, spare parts for

American jet fighters, and other sensitive military equipment for its war against Iraq.

The Rafsanjani forces gladly accepted this military aid and helped obtain the release of some U.S. hostages then held in Lebanon. But Rafsanjani was carrying out the policies of Ayatollah Khomeini and other top clerical leaders, not some secret moderate policy that would lead to improved relations with the United States. After the exposure of Iran-Contra, the United States shifted to full support for Iraq in the deadly Iran-Iraq War and dropped all mention of supporting "moderate" Iranian leaders.

Reformists Triumph in 1997 Presidential Elections

U.S. leaders were similarly befuddled by the surprise election of President Khatami in 1997. Promising greater cultural and political freedoms, Khatami prevailed over a badly divided conservative camp. The Clinton Administration was never sure whether to praise or attack Khatami, and eventually did both.

Khatami was elected because Iranians were tired of economic stagnation, official corruption, and harsh cultural and political restrictions. The reformist camp—composed of some former revolutionary student leaders, liberal-minded clergy, professionals, and private-sector businesspeople—tapped a deep vein of discontent among Iranians. In 1997 Khatami won 70 percent of the vote, garnering support across class lines—picking up votes from workers, the poor, and the middle class.

Khatami ran on a platform of promoting civil society and strengthening democracy, and he wanted Iran to rejoin the international community. At the time, he had support of some clergy and conservative politicians, including Rafsanjani and Gholam Hussein Karbaschi, the powerful mayor of Tehran.

If Iran had been a third world dictatorship, the conservative forces who had been in power could have engineered a military coup or other illegal seizure of power. But Iran is no typical third world autocracy. Instead, some bazaaris, conservative clergy, conservatives in the IRGC, and others bided their time. They knew that the president had limited power, and they exploited that to the max.

For example, in the late 1990s, President Khatami wanted to improve relations with the United States. Clinton's Secretary of State Madeleine Albright gave a speech in which, for the first time, the United States expressed mild self-criticism about the 1953 CIA coup against the democratic government of Prime Minister Mohammad Mossadegh. The March 17, 2000, speech made a tepid reference in one paragraph that it had been a mistake for the United States to back the coup, but then it went on to list the many U.S. grievances against Iran.[15] Nevertheless, the Clinton Administration hoped the speech would pave the way for a dialogue with Iranian leaders.

After the speech, President Khatami met with Supreme Leader Khamenei to request that they explore possible improved relations with the United States, according to Rutgers professor Amirahmadi, who later interviewed Khatami. Remember, the Supreme Leader controls foreign policy. Khamenei refused to pursue further openings. If Iran opened talks with the Americans, the leaders would lose support among the army, sectors of IRGC, and conservative clerics, even though they make up a minority of the population. The potential opening with the United States went nowhere.[16]

That one example was repeated on other fields. Khatami al-

lowed much greater press freedom, and the conservative judiciary shut down over a hundred newspapers. Khatami was
the first official in Iran to acknowledge that the ministry of
intelligence was involved in the serial killing of writers.[17] His
government arrested the deputy intelligence minister, who
later allegedly committed suicide in jail. Khatami was blocked
from pursuing a deeper purge of the intelligence services.

Khatami was willing to allow greater freedom of speech for
students, but the intelligence services and Basijis functioned
as a law unto themselves. The Basijis gained fame as shock
troops in the Iran-Iraq War. They morphed into an organized
paramilitary force, enforcing religious edicts such as banning
alcohol and public interaction between unrelated people of
the opposite sex. In an infamous incident on July 8, 1999, intelligence services allied with the Basijis violently assaulted
students in their dorm at the University of Tehran, killing at
least one and wounding dozens.[18]

Khatami, wherever his personal sympathies lay, failed to
respond to these numerous conservative attacks. His failure
to deliver on his promises of reform led directly to the defeat
of his camp in the 2005 elections.

The Conservative Backlash in the 2005 Elections

Late one night, we were caught in a Tehran traffic jam of
honking horns and screaming drivers. Having been born in
Los Angeles, I assumed this was just the Persian version of
road rage. But in fact, we had stumbled upon a campaign
event for Rafsanjani. Young people, faces painted with the
colors of the Iranian flag, were passing out flyers to motorists,
who in turn were honking and expressing their support or
displeasure. Campaign posters hung everywhere.

On another day, as we left Friday prayers held at the University of Tehran, supporters of conservative candidates were passing out leaflets and explaining to the pious why their candidate was best for the Islamic Republic.

The June 2005 elections displayed how a country can have genuinely competitive elections without being democratic. Over a thousand people declared their candidacies for president. The Guardian Council ruled that the vast majority, including all the women, were not sufficiently Islamic. The Guardian Council is a twelve-person, appointed body that can veto any legislation passed by parliament. It expanded its role to include vetting the qualifications of all candidates for national office.

The Guardian Council also initially disqualified a major reformist candidate, Dr. Mostafa Moeen, a former minister in the Khatami government. Supreme Leader Khamenei realized that disqualification of the leader of a significant political trend would be disastrous. He intervened with the Guardian Council, and they relented. Moeen was allowed to run.

It was a fascinating election. Three candidates represented different trends among the conservatives: Mahmoud Ahmadinejad, then the mayor of Tehran; Ali Larajani, the former head of Iranian state TV and later lead negotiator on Iran's nuclear negotiating team; and Mohammad Bagher Ghalibaf, a Revolutionary Guard hero of the Iran-Iraq War and former Tehran police chief. Two major candidates were identified with the reformist trend: Moeen and Mehdi Karroubi, the speaker of parliament from 2000 to 2004. Conservative bazaaris and clergy and the Supreme Leader tended to support Ghalibaf. Rafsanjani assumed he would win, given his tremendous personal financial resources and support from some clergy, private businessmen, and sectors of the state bureaucracy.

Ahmadinejad ran an unusual conservative campaign. He rarely mentioned religion, instead making populist promises to increase subsidies for poor and working-class Iranians. He appealed to conservative cultural values by denouncing the evils of drugs and prostitution. In thinly veiled attacks on Rafsanjani, he denounced wealth and corruption. Ahmadinejad had backing from the IRGC, bazaaris, and the Basijis. But the mainstream clerical establishment was wary of his populism. No pollster, analyst, or politician I interviewed gave Ahmadinejad much of a chance.

So most observers were caught off guard when Rafsanjani polled 6.1 million votes and Ahmadinejad got 5.7 million, forcing a runoff election two weeks later.[19] Karroubi, a quirky reformist candidate who came in third, publicly asserted that the vote had been manipulated so Ahmadinejad would come in second. Unable to get the intervention of the Supreme Leader to reverse the fraud, Karroubi said he would have to take his complaint to God.

The reformist camp feared an Ahmadinejad victory, which they saw as a takeover by extreme conservatives affiliated with the IRGC. They tended to vote for Rafsanjani in the second round. The ultraconservative camp, which had a long and testy relationship with Rafsanjani, united behind Ahmadinejad. Ahmadinejad won by 62 percent.

How Much Power Does Ahmadinejad Really Have?

Up close Ahmadinejad doesn't look very threatening. He's short (5'4") with a closely shaved beard speckled with gray. He often wears plain slacks and a zipper jacket or wrinkled sport coat. Although he has a Ph.D. in transportation engineering, he doesn't come off as an intellectual. He rose from an obscure professor to a Revolutionary Guard leader; the Tehran City Council later appointed him mayor. Ahmadinejad is street-smart. He's quick to learn and a good debater. Most of all, said Professor Amirahmadi, the president has charismatic appeal to poor Iranians. "He speaks like them. He dresses like them. He sounds like he's one of them. He's a populist person."[20]

That populism allowed Ahmadinejad to attract support from rural voters, rank-and-file religious conservatives, and working-class and urban poor. His most famous slogan during the 2005 election was "Bring the oil money to the people's table." Partly because of this populism, and partly because Ahmadinejad is not a cleric, the powerful, traditional religious leaders remained suspicious.

For example, early in his term, Ahmadinejad declared that women could attend soccer matches. Previously, governments had ruled it was un-Islamic for men and women to attend sporting events together. Ahmadinejad proposed to allow women into strictly segregated seating as a concession to Iranian soccer mania that reached a crescendo in the months before the 2006 World Cup.[21] Within a short time, ranking religious leaders objected, and Supreme Leader Khamenei asked Ahmadinejad to reverse his decree. The president did so.

Even more significantly, Ahmadinejad had trouble getting key cabinet ministers approved by both conservatives and reformists in the parliament. It took over four months for the Majlis to approve the education, social welfare, and cooperatives ministers. Ahmadinejad had promised during the campaign to clean up corruption in the National Iranian Oil Company. But the parliament rejected his first three nominees for oil minister and finally agreed to the fourth a full six months after the process began.[22]

The traditional clergy doesn't like Ahmadinejad, explained Professor Amirahmadi. "They don't know what to do with him. Khamenei decided to make up with him [because] their base overlaps. They are trying to find a way to get rid of him or make him like them. They are frightened about Revolutionary Guards taking over through him."[23]

In December 2006, Ahmadinejad faced setbacks in the off-year elections for the Assembly of Experts and local city councils. His candidates lost significant ground, as both reformists and traditional conservatives gained. While much of the U.S. media continues to report on Ahmadinejad as if he had the power of a U.S. president, in fact, he—like Khatami—confronted the limits of presidential power in Iran. Iran's Supreme Leader, not the president, controls the military, police, judiciary, and other key institutions.

The Rafsanjani Interview

So whatever happened with our strange 2005 journey to interview Rafsanjani? On a small scale, we experienced the wheeling-dealing and underhanded tactics that pass for politics in Iran's ruling elite. We agreed with Rafsanjani's handlers that Norman Solomon, Sean Penn, and I would have a half-hour sit-down interview with Rafsanjani. We even negotiated the number of questions we would be allowed to ask.

We were ushered into Kakh Marmar (Marble Palace), a former palace of the shah that now houses the Expediency Council, headed by Rafsanjani.[24] Security was tight, and it took us nearly an hour waiting in the line to be searched. We were stalled about another hour as Rafsanjani attended a meeting with supporters, mostly government bureaucrats and influential businesspeople.

Then we got a real surprise. Instead of a half-hour sit-down interview, Rafsanjani and a passel of handlers met us in a hallway. We were allowed a few questions and got some stock answers. The campaign photographers took lots of photos of Rafsanjani standing next to Sean Penn. Those photos appeared on the front pages of several newspapers the next day, and the TV stations ran video as well. Rafsanjani's handlers figured that a photo op with Sean Penn would help attract the youth vote. So, apparently, they never intended to allow a real interview with time for follow-up questions. It was a minor disappointment but, unfortunately, all too typical of how Iran's ruling elite operates.

Many Iranians don't trust their rulers. Successive U.S. administrations have hoped to use that sentiment, find a replacement, and install pro-U.S. elite in their place. And that's what we'll explore in the next chapter.

SIX

Who Will Be Iran's Next Ruler?

For most people in the world, the shah of Iran died in exile in 1980—dethroned and disgraced. But for some Iranian exiles the shah lives—in suburban Washington DC, to be exact. Reza Pahlavi, son of the late shah, was crowned king shortly after his father died. Although he has not set foot in Iran since the 1979 revolution, his supporters still call him "your majesty."

"His majesty is quite busy with interviews and meetings," his assistant told me on the phone when I was attempting to arrange an interview. Once Pahlavi had agreed to meet me, however, apparently his schedule loosened up. "He's free several days next week," she confided in a follow-up call.

One cold morning the assistant picked me up in front of my downtown Washington DC hotel. For security reasons she wouldn't reveal the location of the interview in advance. We drove to the home of Colonel Ovissi in tony McLean, Virginia. The colonel, as everyone called him, originally accompanied Reza Pahlavi to the United States in 1978. His living room was filled with the kinds of carpets, paintings, candle-sticks, and silver cup holders that I recognized from my travels to Tehran. Pahlavi's supporters like to remember their days of glory.

Pahlavi had his own American security man, who had researched me on the Internet before arrival. "You look like your photos," he said casually. Thank God I had current pictures of myself on the Web. The security man carefully searched my briefcase but spared me the indignity of removing my shoes.

At precisely the appointed time, Reza Pahlavi entered the room. He cut a dashing figure, nattily attired in a charcoal pin-striped suit and lavender tie. Born in 1960, his hair is starting to gray but he looks physically fit. He assured me that he wants nothing more than to get rid of the oppressive regime in Iran and allow the people freedom. He talked of democracy, separation of religion and state, and civil liberties. Yet he can't escape the fact that his father and grandfather ran regimes that were far from ideal models of governance. This issue of monarchy versus republican form of government sharply divides the Iranian exile community.

Pahlavi tries to confront the conundrum by saying times are different now. Iranians themselves should choose what system they want. "It's the content of the future system, not its form, that is important," he told me.[1]

In other interviews, he used similar dodges, declining to say what he personally advocates. An hour into our interview, and after considerable pushing, he finally admitted that he wants a constitutional monarchy to replace the current government.

"I happen to believe that system is still a valid option for Iran, and we'll do better to have institutionalized democracy in my country than a republican system. That's my personal opinion. . . . If I didn't believe that, my entire course of action would have been different for twenty-seven years. The reason I don't discuss it is because I don't think it's a healthy debate to argue about the form."[2]

The monarch should represent the nation and not get involved in day-to-day policy making, he told me. But the shah should, under extreme circumstances, be able to dissolve parliament.

Pahlavi clearly wants to return to the throne of his father and grandfather. Thousands of exiled businesspeople, professionals, and others support him as a future king. The United States has kept him in the wings for a possible return to power. He travels the world seeking support.

The United States is always *trying* to find a new ruler for Iran, according to Paul Pillar, CIA national intelligence officer for the Near East and South Asia from 2000 to 2005. U.S. officials pursue "anything that looks like a potential shortcut to political change that would allow us to parachute someone into power," he told me.[3] That vision "continues to have attraction, even if there's no one figure out there.

"The imperial regime under his father and grandfather was not a popular movement or ever had a large amount of popular support," Pillar said. "The same issues that gave rise to the revolution in the late 70s are ones that would strongly counteract any move by the young shah to gin up a movement in Iran today."

Of course, that's not how Pahlavi sees it.

The Inheritor of a Three-Thousand-Year Dynasty?

His supporters claim Pahlavi has significant support inside Iran as the inheritor of three thousand years of imperial history. In fact, his grandfather, Shah Reza Pahlavi, was a military officer who seized power and got himself crowned king in 1925. His original name was Reza Khan, and he simply appropriated the name Pahlavi. At times Reza Shah stood up to Britain and took steps to modernize the country. But Britain and the Soviet Union forced Reza Shah to abdicate in 1941, fearing that his official neutrality in World War II was a cover for pro-German sympathies. His son, Mohammad Reza Pahlavi, was crowned shah that same year.

By the early 1950s, a popular, democratic movement led by Prime Minister Mohammad Mossadegh diminished the power of the new shah. After the CIA and British government engineered a reactionary coup against Mossadegh and restored the shah to full power, the shah became notorious for his brutal, authoritarian rule. So Reza Pahlavi did not inherit a three-thousand-year dynasty but an sixty-four-year family dictatorship.

Reza Pahlavi, of course, strongly disagreed with that characterization of his family. But he said setting the historical record straight could take days. Besides, that's all in the past, he told me. "I'm my own man. This is my vision. It's not based on what my predecessors have or have not done."

But the past is very relevant because Pahlavi echoes key political views of his forebears. During the 1950s, his father used anti-communism to justify repression. The supposed threat of a Soviet takeover of Iran was the excuse.

Immediately after World War II, the Soviet Union, as well as Britain, had troops stationed in Iran. The USSR supported the Tudeh (communist) Party and briefly backed the establishment of independent Kurdish and Azerbaijani states led by leftists. The Soviet Union withdrew its troops from Iran, however, and by the early 1950s posed no threat of invasion. The shah continued to use the excuse of a Soviet takeover to crush opposition, much like other U.S.-backed anti-communist regimes throughout the region. Even today, Pahlavi blames the USSR for not allowing Iran to modernize and become a bastion of civil liberties.

"At the time, there was a Cold War," he said. "That was a major issue undermining our ability as a country to fulfill the goals we had in terms of liberalization. Most of the problems that occurred in terms of restricting political freedoms were directly related to elements that were pretty much doing the bidding of the Kremlin, in the form of the Tudeh Party and some other leftist groups."

In fact, the Tudeh and other leftist parties, whatever their long-term objectives, backed the nationalist forces seeking democratic reform. The shah used anti-communism as the excuse for brutal repression to keep himself in power, along with U.S. and British oil interests.

Pahlavi offered this decidedly un–civil-libertarian explanation for his father's repression and how innocents were caught in a repressive net: "It's almost like tuna fishing and a lot of innocent dolphins get caught in the middle. And that is something that frustrates, or puts a dent into, the liberalization program." Pahlavi clearly sees himself as the fisherman, not the dolphin.

The Terrorist Threat Replaces Anti-Communism

These days, Reza Pahlavi uses the terrorist threat as his father once used the communist threat. He asserted, in a wonderfully mangled metaphor, that Iran is the major source of terrorism in the world.

"You have been dispatching your fire trucks all over the world, trying to put out fires lit by these terrorists. But have you once gone after the guy with matches in his hand? Who is the chief arsonist in all this? The head of the octopus is Tehran."

Well, actually, it's not. Iran backs armed groups such as Hizbollah in Lebanon and Hamas in Palestine. Those groups have carried out armed attacks on civilians. But Iran strongly opposes Sunni groups such as Al Qaeda and the Taliban in Afghanistan. Pahlavi and successive U.S. governments intentionally mislead the public about terrorism by lumping together disparate groups that have little in common politically.[4] In our interview, I pushed Pahlavi about how he could say Iran supports violent, Sunni groups.

"We say the wolf is the brother of the jackal.... I'm not saying what is represented by bin Laden is from the Islamic Republic [of Iran], but at the end of the day, when you look at the regime in Iran, it has been a source of backing and support."

In fact, there is no credible information that Iran is backing bin Laden. The Bush Administration used similar misinformation to scare the American public into supporting the 2003 U.S. invasion of Iraq. Saddam Hussein was an evil dictator, but he wasn't supporting Al Qaeda.

Pahlavi's biggest problem is that he has no political base inside Iran. In three trips to that country, I met virtually no one who favors the return of a constitutional monarchy. The shah's supporters can't point to any significant organizations or movements inside Iran that champion their cause. Iranians have a strong memory of the Pahlavi dynasty, and no sweet words from the young shah will alleviate their fears.

As former CIA officer Pillar told me, Pahlavi can't lead a

movement of any political significance. "I suspect he and his supporters, . . . with each passing month and year, are getting progressively more out of touch with the realities back in their homeland."

Before the 2003 invasion of Iraq, the Pentagon and neoconservatives promoted Ahmad Chalabi as the future ruler of Iraq. Chalabi even met with international oil companies to discuss allocation of Iraq's future production. But after the invasion, Chalabi proved to be far more unpopular than his backers ever imagined. In 2005 Chalabi couldn't even get elected to parliament. Unwilling to learn the lessons of Iraq, however, U.S. officials continue the search for a pro-American Iranian leader.

Waiting in the Wings but Reluctant to Go on Stage

Mohsen Sazegara has the kind of pedigree treasured in Washington. He was an aid to Ayatollah Khomeini and helped found the Revolutionary Guard in the early years of the revolution. He broke with the government in 1989, becoming an outspoken critic of the government and an editor of reformist newspapers. Imprisoned for his political views, Sazegara suffered eye problems and was eventually allowed to leave Iran for medical treatment.

In 2004 Sazegara became known for helping organize a petition drive to hold a referendum for a new Iranian constitution. Patrick Clawson, a hardliner who is deputy director for research at the Washington Institute for Near East Policy, brought Sazegara to Washington.[5] Sazegara has held various academic posts in the United States in recent years and resided at Harvard University in 2007.

Sazegara's history, liberal views, intimate knowledge of the Revolutionary Guard, and insights into splits within Iran's ruling elite make him appealing to sectors of the U.S. ruling circles. Sazegara isn't getting with the program, however. He doesn't agree with Bush Administration hardliners, who continually threaten military action against Iran. Sazegara favors negotiations, and he warns U.S. authorities not to anoint anyone as a single leader of the opposition movement.[6]

So the search continues.

In 2006, neoconservative and former Pentagon advisor Richard Perle offered support to a recently exiled political prisoner named Amir Abbas Fakhravar. Perle claimed that Fakhravar was a well-known student leader who escaped from the infamous Evin prison and then secretly fled from Iran to the West. Fakhravar ended up testifying on Capitol Hill and was invited to attend a meeting of Iranian exile leaders at the White House.

Unlike Sazegara or former political prisoner Akbar Ganji, Fakhravar seems to echo the neoconservative views on Iran. He told *Mother Jones* magazine that "any movement or any action whatsoever" by the United States would "help or enhance the people to rise up."[7] But Fakhravar's star dimmed as his connections to neoconservatives became more apparent, and the exile community questioned his bona fides as a student leader. Several former student activists said they had never heard of him when he was supposedly leading the student movement in Iran.

U.S. Conservatives Support a Cult

Some conservatives have thrown support behind an even stranger ally: the People's Mujahideen of Iran (Mujahideen-e-Khalq, or MEK). The MEK began in the 1970s as an organization combining leftist and Islamic ideologies to fight the shah. The MEK bombed U.S. and Iranian targets during the 1970s, killing U.S. citizens. The State Department lists the MEK as a terrorist organization.[8]

The MEK developed a significant base of support in Iran immediately after the revolution, but it suffered extreme repression by the government and eventually moved its headquarters to Iraq, which was at war with Iran. This alliance with the hated Saddam Hussein embittered most Iranians and largely eliminated whatever respect the MEK may have won from its earlier resistance.

After the 2003 U.S. invasion of Iraq, the United States allowed the MEK to keep its small arms and control its own military base, originally established by Saddam's officials. The United States has not officially allowed the MEK to attack Iran and instead developed a work-around. Members need only declare that they have left the MEK and now support democracy. The United States then uses them for armed attacks inside Iran.[9]

Ideologically, the MEK has renounced its leftist history, and it claims to favor free markets and democracy. But critics question that commitment, given the cult of personality built around MEK's two leaders, Masoud and Maryam Rajavi. MEK members must hold the leaders in adulation and shun contact with outsiders—even other anti-Iranian government activists. Former MEK members allege that the MEK separates children from their families and trains them as guerrilla fighters.[10] "They are easily categorized as a cult," Massoud Khodabandeh, a former MEK member now living in London, told me.[11]

Nevertheless, prominent American conservatives such as

Florida Republican Representative Ileana Ros-Lehtinen have long supported the MEK as a legitimate alternative to the current government.

Abraham Sofaer, a top State Department official from 1985 to 1990, and now George Schultz, senior fellow at Stanford's conservative Hoover Institution, said both Clinton and Bush administrations have tried to overthrow the Iranian government by backing dissident organizations. "The U.S. has supported groups opposed to the Iranian government," he told me. "It hasn't worked for years."[12]

So, divided among themselves and lacking credible choices, U.S. officials continue the search for an Iranian Idol. And what could be a more appropriate locale than a city near Hollywood?

Monarchists in Tarzana

The San Fernando Valley area of Los Angeles is best known for shopping malls and valley girl lingo. Now the valley town of Tarzana has another claim to fame. The city is home to a bevy of monarchists intent on reclaiming the glory days of the shah. And they are intent on using their Farsi-language TV stations to promote the future rulers of Iran.

Take a drive north on the 405 freeway from west Los Angeles toward Van Nuys. A few exits later sits Tarzana, originally a working-class suburb that still has lots of low-rise warehouses. It really was named after Tarzan—a tribute to the city's native son and Tarzan author, Edgar Rice Burroughs. Drive less than a mile from the freeway, past the Red Barn Feed and Pet Food store and a self-storage outlet, and a nondescript warren of small offices pops up. Inside sit the offices of PARS TV and AFN TV. Just down the road, in Canoga Park, sits a third TV station, Channel One.

These and other Los Angeles TV stations broadcast via satellite to North America, Europe, and Iran. I watched several of the LA stations while in Tehran one evening. They appear to be big-time operations. A commentator sits behind an expansive news desk. His fax machine is in plain view, reminding viewers they can fax their comments any time. An impressive array of graphics appears behind the commentator, perhaps a famous Tehran monument or a rippling Iranian flag.

But viewed from inside the studio, the sets look considerably less impressive. The production values are limited. A commentator with a few notes sits in front of a green screen. At PARS TV, two scrawny TV cameras and a few lights fill the small studio. Everything is run from a control room about the size of a large walk-in closet. At AFN TV the day I visited, a grand total of two employees were present; one came specifically for the interview with me. The owner doubles as the technical crew.

The stations did share one thing in common. The owners of the top three political TV stations all had pictures of the late Shah Mohammad Reza Pahlavi prominently displayed in their offices. When asked if they were monarchists, all declined to state.

"Of course I have my own view," Shahram Homayoun, president of Channel One TV, told me. He said the issue remains extremely controversial in the exile community. "If I tell you my views, the person who disagrees won't sit next to me."[13]

Many of the LA broadcasters are out of touch with reality, according to Bijan Khalili, owner of Ketab Books and the

Iranian yellow pages phone service. The LA media are so conservative and engage in so much infighting that they have little credibility in Iran. "All the TV stations attack one another," he told me.[14]

Los Angeles became a center for Farsi-language media precisely because so many Iranian exiles came to southern California after the 1979 revolution. They even have a name for it: Tehrangeles.

Tehrangeles Is Born

Iranian students and former students had settled in Los Angeles during the 1960s and 70s. But after 1979, the area saw a huge influx of wealthy businesspeople, former military and intelligence officials, professionals, and ordinary Iranians.

To learn more about Tehrangeles, I didn't have to go far. I just drove back to the neighborhood where I lived as a child. I grew up in a middle-income section of Los Angeles just south of UCLA. I used to walk up Westwood Boulevard toward Westwood Village, past a stockbroker's office and the Crest movie theater.

Today, some forty-five years later, Iranian groceries, bakeries, book stores, and music shops take up nearly every storefront. A New England–style warren of small offices used to house the ultra-right-wing John Birch Society. Today those offices hold Asian and Iranian businesses providing immigration advice and passport photo services. Where white kids in Madras shorts used to tread, Iranians speaking Farsi now stride. And, to tell you the truth, it's an improvement. The neighborhood has more character now. What do you prefer: white bread or saffron rice?

The 2000 census counted 117,000 people of Iranian origin living in southern California and 338,000 nationwide.[15] Critics of the census say those figures are too low because "Iranian" isn't a listed category on the census form. Many Iranians classify themselves as "Caucasian" rather than handwrite "Iranian."

Some of the LA media owners claim the census count is off by a factor of 10. At a million strong, they portray a Persian demographic lion stalking the streets of Tehrangeles. Of course, such claims also bolster efforts to sell ads, particularly to skeptical, non-Iranian companies.

Khalili told me no one has absolutely accurate figures. He offers an educated guess, based on an extrapolation from the number of Iranian surnames in his published phone directories. Khalili estimates three hundred thousand people of Iranian origin live in Los Angeles County, with another hundred thousand in Orange and San Diego counties.[16]

For sure, he said, the exile media claim of one million is highly inflated. But that is far from their only, or even most serious, prevarication.

Bending the Truth Beyond Recognition

Los Angeles now boasts some twenty cable and satellite TV stations broadcasting in Farsi, along with numerous newspapers and magazines and countless Web sites.

Amir Shadjareh, owner of PARS TV in Tarzana, claims his station has 1 million viewers in the USA and Canada, and another 1.4 million inside Iran.[17] Shahram Homayoun, head of Channel One TV, claims a total of 10 million viewers.[18] While the station owners concede that the entertainment stations draw far larger audiences, each claims to have the largest number of viewers for a political station. The estimates of Iranian viewership appear to be widely exaggerated; no independent companies can verify them. The number of viewers in the United States is too small for the Nielsen rating service to even track.

Exaggerating their audience size is just the beginning. The conservative exile media also have the unfortunate habit of overestimating their political support inside Iran. One notorious incident in 2005 illustrates the cockeyed contortions of both the conservative opposition forces and their supportive media. It was something right out of the Keystone Kops.

On May 27, 2005, the Hakha Movement issued a press release announcing an upcoming press conference at the National Press Club in Washington DC. Hakha is a cultlike organization, centered around its leader, Ahura Pirouz Khaleghi Yazdi, with a satellite TV program in Virginia. In the press release, Yazdi said Iranian mullahs must "hand over the government to the people of Iran before or on June 16, 2005, at 10:00 a.m. Tehran time. Otherwise, like a swift-moving hurricane, the People of Iran will stand united and will force the mullahs to give up their power and leave the country."[19] Yazdi was going to personally fly to Tehran to oversee the uprising.

This press release was treated seriously by some of the conservative exile media, with excerpts still posted on Web sites and in blogs.[20] On the appointed day, Yazdi and some followers appeared on Hakha TV calling for massive demonstrations to overthrow the regime.

Hakha TV got a call reporting that major Iranian leaders were at the Tehran airport preparing to flee. What should they do? The Hakha programmer instructed them to detain the leaders. A later phone call indicated that the leaders had escaped to southern Iran, and he urged that they be detained there. Of course, none of this ever took place, and Yazdi never set foot in Iran. Iranian exiles suspect that Iranian agents had made the phone calls to make Hakha look silly. That appeared to be the case when excerpts of the show were broadcast on Iranian state TV and reprinted in a daily newspaper the next day.

When groups such as Hakha are treated seriously by the exile media, it destroys their credibility inside Iran. Iranians like to watch the exile stations that broadcast music and entertainment. But the political stations' reputation is so bad that, during street interviews, some Iranians asked me if the people on air were really Iranian.

The exile media have also become famous for distorting their news accounts to promote a cause. In May 2006, Amir Taheri, a neoconservative columnist for the *National Post* of Canada, wrote that Iran's Majlis had passed a law requiring Jews to wear a yellow stripe on their clothing. Christians and other minorities would be forced to wear distinctive badges as well.

Wire services and other mainstream media quickly picked up the story as an example of the Iranian government's rampant anti-Semitism. However, reporters, including those from the Jewish press in the United States and Canada, quickly discredited the story by simply looking up the Majlis debate and legislation online. Majlis members, including Jewish members of parliament, flatly denied the story. Iran had passed a law encouraging Iranians to wear traditional Iranian clothing, but there was no mention of special dress or markings for re-

ligious minorities.[21] The *National Post* quickly retracted the
story and issued an apology a few days later.[22]

Nevertheless, the LA exile media continued to play the
story for weeks. When asked about his inaccurate coverage of
the issue, Channel One owner Homayoun insisted to me that
the story was valid. "That story wasn't untrue," he insisted.
Iranian officials "floated it to see how people would respond.
The minority leaders in the parliament are paid by the government. So you can't trust what they say."[23]

Homayoun never cited any sources to indicate Majlis
members were "floating a story," and in-depth investigations
of the article found no basis for that claim, which was only
made after the original story proved false.[24]

With each phony or exaggerated story, the LA newscasters
and commentators think they are helping the popular struggle against the Iranian government. But repeated over time,
the distortions discredit the exile media and, by extension, all
the exile opposition.

Abbas Milani, director of the Iranian Studies Program at
Stanford University, told me many Iranians say, "If this is the
alternative to the regime, we don't want this change. Is this
the best the opposition has to offer?"[25]

Where's the Money?

All the exile broadcast owners I interviewed denied receiving
U.S. government funding. But they would all grab some if
they could. In the spring of 2006, owners of the major
Tehrangeles stations met individually with representatives of
the U.S. State Department. Many ended up applying for government money to help their stations.

PARS TV owner Shadjareh told me that he welcomed money for technical support, such as getting his network onto Hotbird, the most popular satellite broadcasting to Iran and the Middle East. The State Department had a total of $85 million to disburse, mostly for media outlets.

Kazem Alamdari, a sociologist at California State University, Los Angeles, said the LA stations destroyed their own credibility by constantly trying to undercut each other during the State Department meetings. U.S. officials got tired of "these TV stations attacking each other," said Alamdari.

The State Department has publicly announced that it is spending $50 million to beef up its own media, including the satellite TV version of Voice of America. The United States is also upgrading Radio Farda, the Iranian equivalent of Radio Free Europe.[26]

If the U.S. government was truly interested in supporting democracy in Iran, it wouldn't have to look far to find legitimate opposition movements inside Iran. The people of Iran are angry. Some are fighting the clerical government. But as we'll see in the next chapter, they're not real fond of U.S. policy.

SEVEN

Iran's Democratic Opposition

The winter snows hit Tehran in late November and only got worse as winter wore on. The already clogged traffic crawled at an even slower pace. Taxi drivers cursed other drivers, as if somehow they had never seen sleet and snow before.

The evening air was dropping toward freezing as I walked down the flight of stairs to Shirin Ebadi's office in a middle-class neighborhood. She is perhaps the best-known human rights activist in Iran, having won the Nobel Peace Prize in 2003. The prize is sometimes awarded in hopes the winners will help bring peace and justice to their homeland in the near future. But in the case of Iran, justice remains some years away.

Ebadi sat in a simple, four-room office filled with books, files, and old photos. One shows Ebadi as a beautiful young woman wearing a head scarf. She is perhaps twenty years older now, but still wears her scarf back on her hair as she did in the photo. Ebadi is tired after a long day of work, but she remained upbeat.

In mid-2006, Interior Ministry officials tried to shut down her Center for the Defense of Human Rights. But international pressure, including a support letter from nine Nobel Peace Prize winners, forced them to back off.[1] Ebadi told me ministry officials later called the attempted closing "a misunderstanding." But Iran's ubiquitous security services continued to tap her phone and watch her office. She has received anonymous death threats.

Ebadi explained that by the end of 2006, the popular resistance to the government was more muted than in years past. In part, Iranians were disillusioned with the failure of the reformists such as President Khatami to deliver on their promises. And in part, the security forces under President Ahmadinejad had cracked down even harder than in previous years.[2]

Ebadi and other human rights activists are at the forefront of promoting democracy and civil society. And, significantly, they all oppose U.S. meddling. In fact, they say, the United States makes matters worse. When Congress and the Bush Administration allocate money to "promote democracy" in Iran, that gives the repressive forces in Iran an additional excuse to crack down on the opposition, claiming they are tools of the United States.[3]

Akbar Ganji, a leading dissident journalist, told me, "The U.S. money is no good."[4] During my first two visits to Iran, Ganji was held in Evin prison for having published investigative articles showing the intelligence services participated in the murder of four activists and writers in 1998, something later acknowledged by President Khatami. He went on numerous hunger strikes. I had hoped to interview him, but that proved impossible. Activists inside Iran and internationally had turned his imprisonment into a cause celebre and organized a large movement for his release. In 2006 he was freed after serving his six-year sentence. International pressure made sure he wasn't arrested again, and Ganji left Iran.

In person Ganji was much shorter than I imagined. Standing perhaps 5'3", with a receding hairline and thin beard, he looked like a college professor. In exile, various political groups courted Ganji. U.S. officials even offered him a visit to the White House, but Ganji refused. "The U.S. attempt to support so-called democracy is counterproductive," he told me.[5]

The Opposition Says the Nukes Issue Is Phony

Iranian political activists criticize U.S. attempts to use the nuclear issue. U.S. officials scare Americans and Europeans with nightmares of a nuclear-armed Iran. But focusing on the nuclear issue has the opposite effect inside Iran. Iranians see their government under attack from a foreign power. "Americans shouldn't start a military attack," said Ebadi. "And they shouldn't interfere with the internal affairs of the country."[6]

During three visits to Iran, from 2000 to 2006, I conducted many dozens of random interviews with ordinary Iranians. Nearly all of them supported the Iranian government position on nuclear power. That's partly because people receive a heavy dose of government propaganda, and it's partly a nationalist rejection of foreign interference.

Ali Mohammadi owns a small grocery store in a working-class neighborhood of south Tehran. "Iran's nuclear power isn't for mass destruction," he told me. "The American government doesn't want any country to have access to technology or become developed. America just wants everything for itself."[7]

Ganji told me that most Iranians resent the hypocrisy of the U.S. position on nuclear weapons. "If Israel, the United States, Russia, Pakistan, and China have the right to a nuclear bomb, Iran must have that same right," he told me. "If Iran doesn't have the right to a nuclear bomb, then no one has that right." But Ganji said, given the reality of international relations, he opposed all nuclear programs in Iran. "Because there are all manner of dangers facing Iran, I am against this program."

Ebadi said activists in Iran don't separate the issue of nuclear power/nuclear weapons from the issue of democracy. "The government of Iran claims it does not want to make nuclear bombs," she said. "But the international community doesn't believe Iran. What's the solution? Iran isn't a democratic country. And all the decisions are made behind closed doors. The international community can't trust such a government. If the government wants the international community to believe in what it says, it should try to bring real democracy into the country. The political solution to the nuclear energy issue is democracy in Iran."

Ebadi and Ganji are only the most recent in a long line of dissident voices in postrevolutionary Iran who don't align themselves with foreign powers. These opposition movements have ebbed and flowed over the years, but never stopped.

A Short History of Opposition Movements

In 1979 the people of Iran overthrew the hated shah in a genuinely popular uprising. Conservative religious forces led by Ayatollah Khomeini, nationalists, leftist Muslims, and secular Marxists all joined together in hopes of building a new, democratic Iran. In January 1980, in a very competitive election, Iranians elected Abolhassan Banisadr as president with 76 percent of the vote. He was a popular, leftist Muslim who opposed many of the religious conservatives' policies of repression.

The student seizure of the U.S. Embassy in Tehran in November 1979 and then Saddam Hussein's invasion of Iran in September 1980 added to the country's turmoil. The conservative Islamic forces took advantage of the war to intensify attacks on other supporters of the revolution, killing and jailing thousands of nationalists, Marxists, and leftist Muslims. The Majlis impeached Banisadr on phony charges, and he was forced to flee the country in 1981. Repression continued against opposition groups throughout the 1980s, including murders of Marxists and brutal repression of Kurdish rebels fighting in the northwest of the country.

In 1988, in the final days of the Iran-Iraq War, the People's Mujahideen of Iran (Mujahideen-e-Khalq, or MEK) launched an attack on Iran from Iraq in an ill-fated attempt to seize power. The Iranian forces easily beat them back and then launched horrific retaliation inside Iran. Intelligence and judiciary officials murdered as many as 3,800 political prisoners held in jails around the country. Prisoners were asked a series of questions to test their loyalty, including whether they would walk across minefields. If they answered no, they were executed.[8]

Government crackdowns of the 1980s effectively eliminated much of the organized opposition that had hoped to bring real democracy to Iran. But a new generation of activists came of age in Iran and participates in a number of important mass movements.

The Students Rebel

Iran's student movement has played an important role at critical junctures in recent Iranian history. In the period leading up to the 1979 revolution, Muslim and leftist students held significant demonstrations against the shah. The student seizure of the U.S. Embassy served as a catalyst for Khomeini's consolidation of power. After Khomeini's death in 1989, the national Muslim student association became more critical of the government, which foreshadowed the rise of the reformist trend in the 1990s.

Iran has become a nation of young people: 46 percent are below the age of fifteen; 65 percent are below twenty-five. Iran has a sophisticated system of higher education, but many young graduates can't find work. Unemployment runs an estimated 16 to 20 percent among youth. Conservative clerical forces feared the growth of a genuine democratic trend among Muslim students. Using the judiciary and intelligence services, they cracked down hard on student protests.

In 2000 I walked into a nondescript building near the University of Tehran campus. The furniture was threadbare. The whole office needed a fresh coat of paint. But the file cabinets looked familiar. They were U.S. government issue, taken from the U.S. Embassy during the 1979 takeover. We were visiting the Office for Strengthening Unity (OSU), Iran's main student organization at the time. The OSU had acquired the file cabinets when it was a staunch supporter of the Islamic government. But since 1989, it had become part of the Islamic opposition.

Journalists Keith Porter, Maziar Bahari, and I had just arrived to interview a top leader of Iran's student movement, Ali Afshari. We were preparing an hour-long radio documentary, *The Struggle for Iran*, hosted by Walter Cronkite.[9] Afshari wanted the Islamic state to continue but favored elimination of the ruling elite's privileges. "We need a wider distribution of wealth and more social justice," he told us. He stressed that Iranians should be able to have different interpretations of Islam. "We believe that religion can function in the framework of democracy."[10]

He, like other student leaders, strongly criticized U.S. policy toward Iran. "For over fifty years America has worked to weaken democracy in Iran. The United States must remove forces from the Persian Gulf and remove the sanctions against Iran. America must acknowledge our right to sovereignty."

About a month after our interview, Afshari was arrested for speaking at a large student meeting and accused of "spreading propaganda" against the Islamic Republic. Afshari was tortured into giving a false confession, was sentenced to three years in prison, and later went into exile.[11]

When Ahmadinejad became president in 2005, the repression worsened. The new president barred students from inviting prominent reformists to speak on campus, banned certain student publications, and purged liberal faculty at major universities.

Some students fought back. In an action that gained international publicity in December 2006, students heckled Ahmadinejad, who was speaking at Amirkabir University. They held his photo upside down and forced him to cut short his speech. Students expressed anger at the lack of civil liberties, but also at the high cost of education and the lack of jobs after graduation. And for the first time during his administration, they shouted "Death to the dictator."[12]

The Iranian student movement is far from dead.

The Women's Rights Battle

Westerners often confuse the status of women in Iran with their status in fundamentalist-led Arab countries. They see photos of Iranian women clad in the black chador and assume the worst. The Iranian government, in its defense, notes that Iranian women are far freer than in U.S.-supported Arabic countries. In Saudi Arabia, for example, women can't vote or even get driver's licenses. In Iran, women make up over 60 percent of university students, and they hold high-level jobs in universities, medical fields, and government.

Iranian females are indeed freer than women in Saudi Arabia, Kuwait, and Afghanistan. But in the view of many Iranian women, that's not enough. Take the issue of the chador. Women have worn the chador for centuries as part of their religious and cultural tradition. Many women, particularly those in rural areas, would choose to wear it even if no government dress code existed.

But after Ayatollah Khomeini consolidated his power in the 1980s, the government forced women to wear very conservative dress. Those who were caught on the street without proper attire could be arrested and whipped. Yet younger women in particular continued to rebel against these restrictions, allowing bits of hair to peek out from the hijab and taking other risks. Women spearheaded a similar informal rebellion against rules prohibiting unrelated men and women from being together in public.

President Khatami, elected in 1997, responded to pressure from the women's movement and considerably relaxed cultural restrictions. Today in major Iranian cities, some young women wear jeans with manteaus and head scarves pushed far back on their hair. Women are still not free to dress as they please, but popular opposition forced significant changes.

The battle for women's rights continues because Iran's interpretation of Islam institutionalizes a great deal of discrimination and oppression. One afternoon I visited the apartment of Pouran Farrokhzad—a writer, women's rights activist, and sister of Iran's most celebrated woman poet, the late Forough Farrokhzad. In the 1960s and 70s, poet and filmmaker Forough Farrokhzad wrote openly about femininity, sex, and other controversial issues that make her a heroine to the women's rights movement today.[13] Her sister continues the struggle.

"Women are still considered half a man in this country," Pouran Farrokhzad told me emphatically.[14]

In the case of an auto accident or other civil matters, for example, Iranians may be required to make a payment to the injured party in what's known as "blood money." Farrokhzad described a recent case of a family seeking compensation for the life of their relative who died in an accident. "A pregnant woman carrying a male child died recently. The boy baby inside her womb carried twice the blood money as her. You can see how painful these rules and laws are."

Under Iran's interpretation of Sharia law, "crimes against chastity" (adultery, sex before marriage) are illegal. Adultery can be punished with death. A British television documentary exposed the hanging of a sixteen-year-old Iranian girl for "crimes against chastity," although she had been raped by a married man three times her age.[15] In cases of rape or other sex-related offenses, men are likely to go free or receive lighter sentences.

Farrokhzad said, "We live in a very bizarre era. Our lives

are like a river. The religion puts a dam to block this river. If this dam is removed, we continue our way and show our true face to the world."

The women's movement had launched a strong campaign against the government's policy of execution by stoning. The Iranian judiciary continued to approve death by stoning for those convicted of adultery and other crimes. At the end of 2006, nine women and two men were awaiting death by stoning.[16]

Women's organizations attempted to hold two peaceful demonstrations in 2006, demanding equal rights for women. As women showed up in a major Tehran square, "police attacked women and beat them," Ebadi told me. "One woman ended up with a broken arm. About seventy people were arrested. Some were in jail for one month. One man spent four months in jail."

In late 2006, nongovernmental organizations (NGOs) in Tehran initiated a campaign to gather one million signatures in support of women's rights. The petition demanded full equality for Iranian women. Organizers gathered signatures door-to-door and on the Internet.[17]

Such campaigns indicate the Iranian government has been unable to crush dissent. "The culture of the Iranian people doesn't allow the government to drag the country backward," said Ebadi. "Maybe the government wants it, but the culture doesn't allow it."

Wildcat Strikes and Independent Unions

While the student and women's movements tend to get more publicity in the West, anger also simmers below the surface among working-class Iranians. In recent years official unemployment has hit 11 percent and inflation 13.5 percent. The real figures are probably higher. The Islamic government created pro-government trade unions, but they frequently fail to represent workers' interests. So workers have launched numerous demonstrations and wildcat strikes, in some cases led by independent Marxists.

In December 2005 Tehran bus drivers demanded higher wages, improved working conditions, and an independent union. They refused to collect passengers' tickets, as a pressure tactic on the city-owned bus company. When their leader, Mansour Ossanlou, and others were arrested, workers held a wildcat strike. That was only the most widely publicized of numerous spontaneous worker actions around the country.

The bus drivers' strike "was an important incident," Ganji told me. "The workers have legitimate concerns. They were demanding minimum pay and that they should be paid back wages that the government had refused to pay. Their demand was primarily of a trade union type. But because there is such extensive repression in Iran, every trade union demand ultimately becomes political."

Shirin Ebadi confirmed that "the protests are about economic issues. But the economic problems of people in this country are rooted in the political problems. Iran is a rich country. If the people are poor, it's because of the wrong policies of the government and corruption."

NGOs Try to Create Civil Society

I was surprised when I got off an elevator at an upper floor of a downtown Tehran office building. I had to step around a group of Arab-Iranian women sitting on the floor. The women had come to the office of the Institute to Defend Prisoner's Rights because their male relatives had been convicted of carrying out terrorist bombings in Ahvaz, a southern city with many Arab-Iranians. Their visit to this NGO was a last-ditch effort to gain international attention and stop the men's executions.

Institute director Emad Baghi weaved in and out of the fifty people camped out in his office, offering advice and sometimes stopping to answer phone calls from major politicians. He was trying desperately to get the executions postponed. Baghi and his committee carried out the sometimes lonely fight for civil liberties and against the death penalty in a country that executed some ninety-four people in 2005.[18]

People such as Baghi and Shirin Ebadi dedicate their lives to running nongovernmental organizations, a type of nonprofit group. They focus on human rights and civil society issues without directly participating in elections or similar political activities. The government regularly cracks down on NGOs but must often back off because the UN, human rights, and other international groups protest against the repression.

The progressive NGOs helped to create space for a wider opposition movement.

The United States Sponsors Terrorism

The United States claimed to support the opposition movements in Iran, while clandestinely promoting terrorist attacks. And I don't use the term loosely. Terrorism is the intentional killing or injuring of innocent civilians for political ends. Recent actions inside Iran certainly fit that definition.

Sometimes the perpetrators are unknown; other times they fit the classic pattern of U.S. black operations.

In June 2005 a bomb exploded in a main square in Tehran, injuring several passersby. Then in 2005 and 2006, at least twenty people died and ninety were injured in bombings in the southern province of Khuzistan, where Iran's Arab minority is concentrated. The Iranian government convicted twenty-three ethnic Arab men and sentenced nineteen of them to death for planting the bombs, claiming they had assistance from British intelligence.

Baghi of the Institute to Defend Prisoner's Rights took up the men's cases as a protest against capital punishment. Baghi admitted to me, however, that ten of the men did plant the bombs and filmed the explosions for propaganda purposes; eight others purchased bomb-making supplies but didn't use them. Baghi thinks the men were influenced by Arabic satellite TV channels advocating separatism for Khuzistan.[19]

In February 2007, bombs destroyed a bus carrying Revolutionary Guards in the southwest province of Balouchistan. A total of eleven people were killed, and over thirty soldiers and civilians were wounded.[20] The antigovernment Baluchi group Jondollah Organization of Iran officially claimed credit for the attacks.

ABC News aired a report in April 2007 revealing U.S. support for these terrorist attacks. The United States funds Iranian exiles, who in turn provide money to Jondollah leader Abdel Malik Regi. ABC reported, "Regi claims to have personally executed some of the Iranians. 'He used to fight with the Taliban. He's part drug smuggler, part Taliban, part Sunni activist,' said Alexis Debat, a senior fellow on counterterrorism at the Nixon Center."[21]

Seymour Hersh, writing in *The New Yorker*, confirmed that the United States sponsors similar terrorist attacks in other parts of Iran, as well. "The Pentagon has established covert relationships with Kurdish, Azeri, and Baluchi tribesmen, and has encouraged their efforts to undermine the regime's authority in northern and southeastern Iran."[22] In the next chapter, I explain how the United States uses Kurdish guerrillas and the Mujahideen-e-Khalq to carry out such attacks.

These terrorist actions resemble past U.S.-sponsored activities. During the 1980s, the United States trained and financed Sunni fundamentalists to attack Soviet troops and civilians in Afghanistan. The Reagan Administration adopted the same tactics in support of the Contras in Nicaragua. But successive administrations can't seem to learn the lessons of history.

The Impact of U.S. Meddling

Every opponent of the Iranian government that I spoke to criticized the disastrous impact of U.S. policies. When the United States periodically threatens military attacks, funds dissidents, and sponsors terrorism, the administration helps fuel anti-American nationalism, said Ganji. "Passing this [$85 million] budget has made our work much more difficult and the work of the democratic forces much more cumbersome in Iran," Ganji told me.

Shirin Ebadi explained that Iranian activists also opposed unilateral U.S. economic sanctions that began under Jimmy Carter. The sanctions prohibit most trade, investment, and many cultural exchanges.[23] "Economic sanctions hurt people more than the government," said Ebadi. "Americans shouldn't start a military attack. And they shouldn't interfere with the internal affairs of the country."

Iranians rally round their government when faced with an external threat, just as Americans did after September 11, according to former Iranian foreign minister Ebrahim Yazdi. He heads the social democratic Iran Freedom Movement. I met Yazdi at his home in north Tehran. Now in his seventies, Yazdi was the éminence grise of the Iranian opposition. He had a private collection of birds that chirped loudly in the background as we sat down to drink strong, black tea and munch pistachios.

Yazdi told me, "The United States doesn't understand Iran." By threatening possible military action and funding terrorist groups, the Bush Administration tosses a lifesaver to the Iranian government, he said.[24]

Iranians understand that Bush's talk of "democratizing Iran" is code for overthrowing a sovereign government and installing a U.S.-friendly regime, Yazdi said. Iranians went through that experience once with the 1953 CIA coup. "Democracy cannot be imported or exported," said Yazdi. "American soldiers don't carry democracy in their backpacks. It has to come from within."

Leading Iranian activists argue that the United States could play a positive role if it changed policies. The United States should stop focusing on Iran's alleged nuclear program, according to Ebadi. "The Americans should pay more attention to the human rights issues in Iran," she told me. Lest human rights violations also end up as an excuse for future military action, opposition leaders call for joint international activities.

Yazdi said the United States should cooperate with other

countries to hold hearings before the UN's Human Rights Commission and other international bodies. He saw such actions as a tactic to organize international support to strengthen internal opposition, while avoiding unilateral U.S. action. "The U.S. government as an individual member of the UN can back pressure on the Iranian government to observe their human rights obligations as part of a multilateral effort," he said.

U.S. policy toward Iran since the 1979 revolution has failed. The United States must radically shift its policies, according to Ganji. "The United States is a superpower using its military power to force its will on the people. Everyone knows I oppose the Iranian regime. But it is us, the Iranians, who must change it."

As I left Yazdi's home, I bundled up against the cold night air. I walked a few blocks through the quiet neighborhood with satellite dishes sprouting on many buildings. Iran's opposition movements are similar to those dishes. No matter how much the government tries to eliminate them, they sprout right back.

The United States doesn't appear likely to change policy anytime soon. Both Republican and Democratic leaders prefer to fish in troubled waters. The United States has cast its lines among Iran's volatile ethnic and religious minorities, as we shall see in the next chapter.

EIGHT

Iran's Ethnic Minorities: Rebellion on the Borders

I arrived at the rather large office compound thirty minutes early, having miscalculated the Tehran traffic—again. Dr. As'ad Ardalan hadn't arrived yet, so I hung out on the front porch, raising quizzical looks from the entering officials. When they spoke to me in Farsi, I just nodded my head and hoped they were saying "good morning," rather than "we're calling the Revolutionary Guard, American spy."

When Ardalan arrived exactly on time, we went upstairs to his modest office. He's an ethnic Kurd and a researcher with a major government think tank. But he stressed that he was speaking as an individual.

Ardalan told me that since the 1979 revolution, Kurds in Iran have been considered "second-class citizens. . . . They don't have access to the country's wealth, face discrimination in getting government jobs, and can't learn Kurdish in school. Even when development money is allocated by the central government, the contractors are not Kurdish. So there's a lot of corruption. The money goes back to Tehran, and doesn't stay in the Kurdish region."[1]

Supporters of the Islamic Republic argue that ethnic minorities don't face discrimination. They concede that some minority regions lack economic development, but those problems can be resolved within the country's constitutional system. Ethnic-minority calls for autonomy or federalism will result in separatist movements, the argument goes, and rip apart the territorial integrity of Iran.[2]

So who's right? The answer is crucial to the future of Iran and to U.S. policy. The U.S. government is politically supporting dissident ethnic minorities, and in some cases, sponsoring terrorist attacks inside Iran. Some conservative Americans are openly advocating the breakup of Iran along ethnic lines.

Edward N. Luttwak, a leading conservative military analyst, wrote, "Certainly there is no reason why Iran should be the only multinational state to resist the nationalist separatism that destroyed the Soviet Union."[3]

Meanwhile the Iranian government cracks down on dissenters, causing even greater resentment among the minority peoples. The future of Iran, in no small part, rests in the hands of the country's minorities.

Iranian but Not Persian

Most Americans use the terms *Iranian* and *Persian* interchangeably, as do many Iranian exiles. In fact, Iran is a multi-ethnic country with a greater percentage of minorities than the United States has. Fars (Persians) make up only 51 percent of Iran's 68.5 million people. Azerbaijanis (24 percent), Kurds (7 percent), Arab-origin (3 percent), Baluchis (2 percent), and other minorities make up nearly half the population.[4] The ethnic minorities don't call themselves Persian.

The Iranian government also discriminates against religious minorities. Sunnis, who make up about 9 percent of Iran's population, cannot hold government office; the government won't allow the building of even a single Sunni mosque in Tehran.

The clerical government says Bahais, members of a faith founded in Persia in the mid-1800s, are unprotected infidels. Iranian clerics see Bahais as apostates and tools of foreign imperialist powers. A Bahai holy site in the city of Babol was destroyed in 2004. Some three hundred thousand Bahais live in Iran, and they try to win converts to their religion, which angers the Shiite leaders.[5] Anyone converting from Islam to another religion can face the death penalty. Bahais face systematic discrimination in jobs, education, and political rights.

Anger seethes among Iran's ethnic and religious minorities and periodically boils to the surface. In recent years, Kurds and Azerbaijanis held large, spontaneous demonstrations, which were brutally suppressed by authorities. "The regime is worried," Iran expert at Stanford University Abbas Milani told me. "President Ahmadinejad has traveled to all these peripheral areas to throw money at the problem, money that he doesn't have."[6]

The United States hopes to exploit the Iranian government's vulnerabilities on this issue by supporting various ethnic groups politically and militarily.

The Kurds and Their Way

In the early 1970s I remember attending a forum hosted by the Confederation of Iranian Students in Berkeley. The Iranians introduced a Kurdish speaker dressed in baggy pantaloon pants and a traditional head scarf. He spoke about the oppression of the Kurds and their fight against the shah's regime.

That was my introduction to a people many Westerners have never heard about. I still remember his distinctive clothing and eloquent explanation of Kurdish history. Kurds are a distinct ethnic group, neither Arab nor Persian. The majority of the estimated thirty million Kurds living in Turkey, Syria, Iraq, and Iran are Sunni Muslim, but in Iran 50 percent are Shiite.[7] After World War I, Britain and France carved up the old Ottoman Empire. Oil had supplanted coal as the world's main energy source, and control of Middle East oil became a major colonial concern. The traditional Kurdish homeland contained a lot of oil.

The Western powers and Turkey intentionally drew maps that divided ethnic Kurds into four different countries. Britain and France hoped that, divided and conquered, the Kurds would not rebel. But some Kurds have been fighting for an independent homeland ever since. Most other Middle Eastern peoples have formed their own independent nations, with the notable exception of Palestinians. So, they ask, why not the Kurds? Other Kurds identify strongly with their country of origin and oppose separatism. In practical terms, Kurdish support for independence hinges on how they are treated politically and economically in their home countries.

At the end of World War II, both the USSR and Britain had troops stationed in Iran. Britain wanted to reassert its neo-colonial control while the USSR supported leftist and communist parties hoping to make revolution. It soon became clear that the Iranian Tudeh (communist) Party couldn't lead a successful revolution in all of Iran. But Kurds and Azerbaijanis were angry at their treatment by Britain and the shah.

Both ethnic groups established independent na
led by leftist parties. Iranian troops, with full
ing, crushed those uprisings and reasserted control from
Tehran. Every year, Iranian Kurds still unofficially celebrate
that short-lived Republic of Mahabad.

In 1978 the Kurdish movement came alive once again as
the shah's regime began to crumble. The Kurdish parties
supported the 1979 revolution and at first tried to negotiate
greater autonomy with the central government. Ayatollah
Khomeini ultimately rejected greater local control, fighting
broke out, and he sent troops to crush the Kurds.

The pesh murgas (guerrillas) enjoyed early successes and
considerable popular support, but they ultimately lost to the
superior numbers of soldiers and technology of the central
government. For a better understanding of that era, check out
Iranian director Azizollah Hamidnejad's powerful award-
winning film *Tears of Cold*. It portrays a fictional love affair
between an Iranian soldier and a Kurdish guerrilla.

Reformist President Khatami did try to improve conditions
for Kurds, appointing Kurds to various government posts. He
tried to improve the local economy by creating a "free economic zone" in Sanandaj, the capital of Kurdistan province.
And he implemented long-ignored provisions of the Islamic
constitution that allowed local city council elections.

But Kurdish resentment against Tehran authorities has
continued over the years. During the 2005 presidential elections, first-round voter turnout was only 37 percent in Kurdistan province, which includes other nationalities. In some all-
Kurdish areas, voter turnout was less than 16 percent.[8]

In 2005, spontaneous protests broke out against police bru-
tality in the town of Mahabad. Authorities accused a Kurdish

man of supporting Kurdish autonomy. He "was shot by police, tied to a car and dragged all the way to a police station, where he was allegedly tortured until he died," according to the BBC.[9] People in Mahabad took to the streets. Kurdish political parties quickly got involved and spread the demonstrations to numerous other Kurdish cities.

Foreign journalists aren't allowed to visit the minority areas of Iran to do political reporting. So to find out more about the Kurdish movement, I had to journey to northern Iraq, where the major Kurdish parties have their headquarters.

Iranian Kurds in Iraqi Kurdistan

I jumped on a plane from Tehran's Imam Khomeini airport to Erbil in northern Iraq. The airport, finished in 2004, sparkled with new entry halls, gift shops, and cafes. Unfortunately, officials at this airport were no more used to handling American journalist visas than their compatriots at the old Mehrabad airport in Tehran. It took them forty-five minutes to finish my processing—and I was just leaving!

I arrived in Erbil late at night, hired a taxi, and drove straight through to Suleimanyah, the region's second city. Such a nighttime journey, unaccompanied by an armed convoy, was impossible anywhere else in Iraq. So I was impressed that the Kurdish Regional Government (KRG) was relatively safe and secure.

The KRG has an interesting history. In 1991 the United States declared a no-fly zone in northern Iraq, thus effectively taking that Kurdish region out of Saddam Hussein's control. For twelve years, Iraqi Kurds controlled their own territory under U.S. protection. After the 2003 U.S. invasion, the Kurds formally established the KRG, which functions as a virtually independent country. The KRG allows Iranian Kurdish parties to operate on its soil.

Those parties face a ticklish situation. The KRG maintains good relations with neighboring Iran. Kurdish leaders, including Iraqi President Jalal Talabani, meet regularly with Iranian officials and historically received financial and political support from them. Talabani lived in Iran for years while fighting Saddam Hussein and speaks fluent Farsi. At the same time, KRG officials feel sympathy for the plight of Iranian Kurds. So they have worked out a compromise.

KRG leaders allow Iranian Kurdish parties to have compounds for their followers and to train pesh murga militias so long as they don't carry out armed actions inside Iran. They can quietly organize among Iranian Kurds living in the KRG but cannot hold public events. Two of the Iranian parties abide by the rules while a third does not, largely because it engages in armed actions with U.S. support. But more on that later.

The Democratic Party of Iranian Kurdistan

The oldest and best-known of the Iranian Kurdish parties is the KDPI (Democratic Party of Iranian Kurdistan). I traveled to the KDPI compound outside of Koya, Iraq, about halfway between Suleimanyah and Erbil. We went through a number of KDPI-controlled checkpoints in a maze of six compounds for its leaders and pesh murga. KDPI Secretary General Mustafa Hejri welcomed me into a room with thick carpets on the floor. Hejri wore nicely tailored, Kurdish slacks and jacket with a traditional gray cummerbund wrapped around his waist. He spoke easily in English, although he seemed tired that day. An assistant immediately brought out glasses of strong, black tea.

Hejri explained that the KDPI is the oldest Kurdish resistance party, having led the Republic of Mahabad back in 1945–46. It supported the revolution against the shah in 1979. Hejri and other KDPI leaders were elected to the Majlis but never allowed to serve. When the clerical government failed to respect Kurdish rights, he said, the KDPI led an uprising that didn't completely stop until 1988.

After the end of that unsuccessful rebellion, KDPI faced a lot of repression. Iranian intelligence services assassinated two KDPI leaders in infamous incidents. In 1989 KDPI leader Abdul Rahman Qassemlou was assassinated in Vienna. On September 18, 1992, Iranian Kurdish leader Sadik Sharafkindi and three others were murdered in a Berlin restaurant when they went to meet with Iranian government representatives.

After 1988, according to Hejri, the KDPI shifted tactics to focus on political organizing against the regime. "Strategically we have not opposed armed struggle," he told me. "But for now we believe political activity benefits the party more than armed struggle. Inside Iran we organize people clandestinely. Sometimes we create NGOs. It's very difficult. A lot of our followers and membership are still in jail. Many have been executed."[10]

KDPI began as a leftist party sympathetic to the Soviet Union. Over time, however, it evolved into a democratic socialist party affiliated with the Socialist International. These days it supports federalism. The central government would control international affairs, the military, and treasury. All other government functions would devolve to local ethnic-minority provinces. "The Iranian regime states that federalism will lead to separation," said Hejri. "But I believe that if all the nationalities have a federal system where their rights are respected, they will stay in Iran."

Hejri visited Washington in 2006 to meet with State Department and other U.S. government officials. "We have had contact with Americans for a long time," he said. Hejri and other KDPI leaders deny accepting U.S. financing, although he said KDPI would accept such aid if offered.

Morteza Esfandiari, the KDPI representative in the United States, told me that KDPI had applied to get some of the $85 million allocated to "promote democracy" in Iran, in order to improve its satellite TV station. "We are friends with the United States. What other friends can we find in the world, other than the United States?"[11]

The KDPI opposes U.S. or Israeli military attacks on Iran's nuclear power facilities as counterproductive. "This kind of bombardment cannot change the regime," said Hejri. "And it will give them big propaganda with the Muslim countries. They can gather more support."

In December 2006, the KPDI announced a split in its ranks. Abdullah Hassan-Zadeh led a dissident group that calls itself KDP-I. While at least some of the issues leading to the split focus on personal and internal power issues, the Zadeh group did criticize Hejri for cooperating too closely with the USA.[12]

The Komala Compound

I expected a different political perspective when I visited the Komala compound in Zerguizala village, just a thirty-minute drive from Suleimanyah. In the 1970s, Komala, which means "association" in Kurdish, was the second-largest Kurdish party in Iran and drew inspiration from the ideology of Mao Zedong. At one time, it held sharp differences with KDPI, but at least on major issues, that's hard to find these days.

When I got to their camp, Komala had just finished a major meeting. Its leaders from Iran, Iraq, and western Europe were still gathered at the compound. Komala General Secretary Abdulla Mohtadi welcomed me into a meeting room, speaking flawless English. I was able to spend part of the day with him and later visit Komala's pesh murga training camp.

Like the KDPI, Komala supports federalism, not separatism. It emphasizes political organizing and eschews armed struggle for now. It trains pesh murga for internal security in Iraq but—like the KDPI—doesn't rule out future action in Iran.

Mohtadi told me Komala engaged in armed propaganda from 2001 to 2005, in which guerrillas carried out political organizing while armed. But they didn't clash with Iranian authorities. Since 2005, they have stopped the armed propaganda, according to Mohtadi. "The KRG asked us not to do [armed] incursions," he told me. "We could do much more if we didn't respect their legitimate interests.[13]

Komala now describes itself as a democratic socialist party with aspirations to join the Socialist International. "The Soviet Union and eastern European countries were all failures," said Mohtadi. "We like the Scandinavian model."

Komala also welcomed U.S. financial support while denying it has actually received any. I posed a query to the room full of Komala leaders, many of whom were veterans of the revolutionary movement of the 1970s. "All over the world, supporters of national liberation shout 'Yankee go home.' But here in Kurdistan you yell 'Yankee come here.' Why?"

The room broke out in laughter, and then there was an embarrassed pause. Finally, Mohtadi said, "We're pragmatists." The United States "can't make democracy, but it can topple dictators."

Unfortunately, the United States doesn't just topple dictators, allow free elections, and then go home. It's a lot more complicated. And to understand U.S. policy toward Iranian Kurds, I had to travel high into the Qandil mountains along the Iran-Iraq border.

Finding the Party of Free Life

The green and brown scrub brush covering the earth quickly acquire a thick layer of snow in winter. The majestic Qandil peaks suddenly dip into fertile valleys. In happier times the mountains could provide scenic views for tourists. But these days they make perfect cover for Kurdish guerrillas crossing the border into nearby Iran. AK-47s slung over their shoulders, they dart into Iran for political organizing and clashes with Iranian troops. In May and August 2006, Iranian artillery shelled Kurdish villages in Iraq in retaliation for those guerrilla raids.

KRG authorities say the rugged terrain makes it impossible to locate, let alone control, the guerrillas. But after only two cell phone calls, I arranged to interview the top leaders of PJAK (Party for a Free Life in Kurdistan), the third major trend within the Iranian Kurdish movement. My colleague Yerevan Adham and I drove in his car to the small Iraqi town of Ranya and then, after looking around a bit, found a driver with a four-wheel-drive SUV. He and other local drivers knew the exact location of the guerrilla camps.

Hmmm. If the local drivers know how to find the guerrillas, why can't the KRG?

In reality, KRG officials look the other way when PJAK launches armed incursions into Iran. That's because the guerrillas are "Kurds helping Kurds," Lieutenant Colonel Dennis Chapman told me.[14] He's a U.S. military officer involved in training Iraqi Kurdish troops. He denied any knowledge of U.S. support for the PJAK guerrillas.

I learned from other sources that the United States is funding and training Iranian guerrillas. "The USA funds PJAK," a Kurdish political activist living in exile told me. "It channels the money through Kurdish groups in [Iraqi] Kurdistan." Seymour Hersh wrote an article in *The New Yorker* indicating that PJAK was supported by both the United States and Israel.[15]

Both countries have chosen a strange ally indeed.

The PJAK camps are located in inhospitable terrain. During winter months, the snowy roads are accessible only on foot or by tractor. Luckily the snows hadn't yet blanketed the area, and we drove up easily—if slowly—over winding dirt roads. Suddenly, young women in green pants and the distinctive Kurdish head scarf were walking along the road. They were female guerrillas. PJAK claims its troops are almost 50 percent women.

At the camp, a group of guerrillas welcomed us into a threadbare room with a thin carpet on the floor and a kerosene stove blasting heat. Just then I remembered reports that every year some Kurds die from kerosene fumes leaking from faulty heaters. I looked around the room. There were no windows. So in case of excessive fumes, I would have to make a mad dash to the doorway.

We chatted while waiting for the guerrilla leaders to descend from the mountains. I asked one of the women fighters, a Kurd from Turkey, what they did to stave off boredom. "We watch satellite TV," she said, insisting that they cared only for news programs. After a few more questions from me, she confessed with a shy smile, they also watch American movies. "We like Brad Pitt and Mel Gibson."

I asked what they thought of Sean Penn. They had never heard of him. In fact, they thought I was asking about Sinn Fein, the northern Irish political party.

About four hours after our scheduled interview time, two top PJAK leaders arrived. The party's top leader, Akif Zagros, had recently died in a flash flood, and the new leader from the political bureau introduced himself by his nom de guerre, Zenar Agri. He stood at perhaps 5'5" and was in his forties with prematurely gray hair. He was the very model of a modern commando general. He carried a cell phone, watched satellite TV, and surfed the Internet. He claimed PJAK was leading the struggle against the Iranian regime.

PJAK grew out of, and remains closely affiliated with, the Turkish PKK (Kurdistan Workers Party). The PKK is led by Abdullah Ocalan, who is jailed in Turkey. The U.S. State Department lists the PKK as a terrorist organization,[16] while PKK supporters say the group engages in legitimate armed struggle. At the camp, posters of PKK leader Abdullah Ocalan hung on the wall along with the PKK flag. Many Kurds say the PKK and PJAK operate as a cult built up around Ocalan. PJAK forbids guerrillas to have sex, for example, although I wonder how stringently that's enforced. The nights get pretty cold up there in the Qandil mountains.

Agri assured me that Abdullah Ocalan has developed a new

global ideology for liberation of Kurds and all oppressed people in the world. Every other sentence was studded with references or quotes from Ocalan. He informed me, for example,
that before the PKK, "the Kurds didn't know about their history and how to struggle." Now, under Ocalan's guidance,
Kurds and all people of the world can follow his road to liberation, Agri told me with a straight face.[17]

The United States, PJAK, and MEK

PJAK has earned a certain amount of respect among Kurds as
the only group currently engaged in armed struggle against
Iran. Even rival political leaders admit that some young people are attracted to PJAK's militancy. PJAK claims to have
killed a hundred Iranian soldiers in a hundred separate clashes
in 2006, mostly near the Iraq-Iran border.[18] That's why the
United States secretly supports PJAK. The Bush Administration understands that PJAK isn't capable of sparking a Kurdish uprising, let alone overthrowing the Iranian government.
But it can carry out destabilizing actions that contribute to
that goal.

The administration plays a similar game with the
Mujahideen-e-Khalq (MEK), an Iranian guerrilla group once
allied with Saddam Hussein and now sitting in a base camp in
Iraq. Mujahideen members need only declare that they have
left the group and support democracy; then the United States
uses them for clandestine military actions inside Iran.[19]

Paul Pillar, a former CIA official in charge of Iranian intelligence, called the MEK more of a cult than a legitimate resistance group. "These are not the kind of partners you want
to have," he told me. "We should have no truck with them."[20]

The USA operates with PJAK in a similar way, according to several sources. "The USA uses PJAK to bother Iran," said Iranian analyst Ardalan. "They don't want to upgrade their power, but use them to bother Iran."[21]

The State Department declined my repeated requests for a response to the charges of helping PJAK or the MEK. But PJAK leader Agri flatly denied that his party receives money from the United States or Israel. "But we would welcome American support," he said with a smile.

I really didn't expect a group getting secret U.S. military aid to fess up in an interview. But I was surprised how closely PJAK allies itself with U.S. policy. PJAK stands virtually alone among opposition groups by supporting U.S. attacks on Iran. "We are happy if the United States bombs Iran, because it might change the regime," said Agri. In a region where the United States faces massive setbacks and political isolation, the Bush Administration takes whatever allies it can find.

So do the Israelis.

Kurds Receive Israeli Support

Northern Iraq emits an air of international intrigue. One day on the streets of Suleimanyah, I saw a group of four Americans walking down the main street. They sported civilian haircuts and clothes but admitted to being U.S. military. Later I learned they were Special Forces (Green Berets) engaged mainly in intelligence gathering.

"Suli is like some Balkan city years ago," one U.S. officer told me. "You've got spies everywhere. Everyone wants to know what everyone else is doing."

I stayed one night in the seedy Ashti Hotel, once a hangout

for Saddam's minions. These days it's like something out of a Graham Greene novel. The smoke-filled lobby served as a meeting place for diplomats, businessmen, soldiers, and spies. Men sat around staring at glasses of strong tea. Every now and again, one would pour a bit of tea into his saucer, let it cool, and slurp it down. I met a Kurdish military advisor there, and when the U.S. Army came to escort me for a story on its operations, the Humvees pulled up near the hotel.[22]

Israel participates actively in the intrigue. Mossad agents posing as businessmen set up shop in the KRG soon after the 2003 U.S. invasion. BBC Television discovered Israeli former special forces soldiers training Kurdish security at the new airport near Erbil and also training a special antiterrorism security squad.[23] The Israelis are also helping train PJAK for its armed forays into Iran.[24] But given sentiment among Arabs and Muslims, the Israeli government tries to keep its activities quiet.[25]

Israel historically tried to ally with non-Arabs in the region against Arab countries. In the past, Israel had close ties with the shah of Iran and Emperor Haile Selassie of Ethiopia. In the 1970s and 80s, Israeli-Kurdish relations were cool because the Kurds supported the Palestinians. Israel worked closely with Turkey, which severely oppresses its Kurdish population. All that changed in recent years as Israel focused on Iran as the most significant enemy. Israel now champions the Kurds, causing tremendous friction with its one-time ally, Turkey.

Iraqi Kurdish officials wouldn't comment on the record about relations with Israel. But a Kurdish military advisor and I had a fascinating conversation. I asked him if the Israeli government was training Kurds. He smiled and said, "Israel is a wonderful country." Then he admitted that he visited Israel for training. After a few minutes of discussion, he reached under his shirt to pull out a gold chain with a Star of David attached. The advisor is a Muslim Kurd, but he got it in Israel. "I can't wear this publicly," he says, "But I have it around my neck all the time."

At least some Iranian Kurdish parties appear to have the same smile-and-wink policy toward Israel. American KDPI representative Esfandiari told me, "We recognize Israel's assistance. We have good relations with Israel. The aspiration of Iraqi Kurds is to create a state like Israel."[26]

Azerbaijanis—the Largest and the Least Known

The Kurdish struggle has received lots of world attention over the years. The same can't be said for other Iranian minorities. Azerbaijanis make up almost a quarter of Iran's population, and even more if you listen to Azerbaijani exiled activists.[27] Yet their situation is little known outside the country.

Azerbaijanis are a Turkish-speaking people, almost all Shiites, ethnically the same as people in the nation of Azerbaijan. The provinces with significant numbers of Azerbaianis are in the northwest of Iran. Nationalists often refer to their region as "South Azerbaijan" with the "North" being the former Soviet republic. In return, the Iranian ruling elite periodically talks about the former Soviet republic of Azerbaijan as actually being part of Iran.[28] Aren't ethnic politics fun?

Azerbaijanis are relatively more integrated into Iranian society than other ethnic groups. As Shiites, they don't face the same religious discrimination as Sunni Kurds, for example. Wealthy Azerbaijani traders dominate a sector of the Tehran bazaar. Supreme Leader Khamenei and Ayatollah Moussavi Tabrizi, the former chief justice of Iran's revolutionary courts, and some other leaders are Azerbaijani. But Azerbaijanis can't study their own language in school.

That and other forms of discrimination date back to before 1979. Nasser, an Azerbaijani activist living in the Washington DC area who asked that I use only his first name, told me that as a schoolboy in 1970, he had to pay a fine for speaking Azerbaijani in school. "We had an old saying," he said. "Azerbaijanis had to speak Turkish, pray in Arabic, and write in Persian."

Nasser pointed out that the mullahs spoke Azerbaijani while the shah's officials did not. Initially, that generated support for the clerical revolution. But Azerbaijanis became disillusioned with the system as the new government failed to recognize their language and cultural rights.

The region exploded in May 2006 when the state-owned newspaper *Iran* published an insulting and racist cartoon likening Azerbaijanis to cockroaches. Tens of thousands of people demonstrated in Tabriz and other cities. The government closed the newspaper and jailed the editor and cartoonist. But demonstrations continued. Several thousand gathered in front of the parliament building in Tehran, but security forces prevented them from demonstrating. Over the two weeks of protests, Azerbaijani activists say dozens were killed and hundreds were injured,[29] but local newspapers reported four killed and seventy injured.[30]

In September 2006 activists called for a boycott on the first day of school to protest the prohibition on students speaking in their own language. Some activists said 40 percent of students in Tabriz participated in the boycott, although it's not possible to verify that number. Dozens of organizers were arrested and imprisoned.

By most accounts, Azerbaijanis want to remain part of Iran with expanded political and cultural rights. A sector of Azerbaijani exiles favors federalism, like their Kurdish counterparts. But another sector favors independence and unification with the country of Azerbaijan. Reza Salahshour, the U.S. representative of the World Azerbaijan Congress, told me that "over 75 percent of the [Azerbaijani] people want independence now."[31]

That assertion runs counter to both my interviews, as well as the opinion of many analysts. Nayereh Tohidi, a fellow at UCLA's Center for Near Eastern Studies, wrote, "the overwhelming majority of ethnic rights activists in Iran declare themselves to be against secessionism."[32]

Arabs in Iran?

When word got out that I was writing this book, I was besieged with e-mails and phone calls from Arab-Iranians. As one of the groups most under attack in 2006–07, they felt a particular urgency to get their story told. Many people outside Iran don't even know that roughly 3 percent of Iran's population are of Arab origin. They mostly live in the province of Khuzistan, a center of Iranian oil production located near the Iraqi border in southern Iran. It was one of the poorest Iranian provinces under the shah and remains so today.

Miloon Kothari, a UN human rights investigator, said Iran's general housing situation is better than that of most developing countries because it has few homeless and no large slums. But during a 2005 visit to Khuzistan, he said living conditions in the province lag far behind the rest of Iran. "There are thousands of people living with open sewers, no sanitation, no regular access to water [or] electricity and no gas connections," he said. In addition, he noted that new development projects just outside the provincial capital have displaced "200,000–250,000 people."[33]

In recent years, Khuzistan has seen a reawakening of a movement for national rights. In April 2005 thousands of people demonstrated when a 1999 document surfaced, indicating the central government planned to forcibly relocate Arabs to other parts of Iran and give Persian names to Arab cities. Scores were killed and some 333 more arrested in a brutal government crackdown.[34] The government said the 1999 document was a forgery, but the large-scale demonstrations indicated the Arab population found such threats credible.

Terrorist bombs went off in Khuzistan in 2005 and 2006, and the government convicted nearly two dozen Arab-Iranians of committing the crimes. It sentenced ten to death.[35] The Iranian government claimed some of these Arab-Iranians received terrorist training in southern Iraq, which is controlled by the British.

Most Arab-Iranian groups oppose separatism. Numbering only about two million and located next to volatile Iraq, Khuzistan residents would have a tough time surviving as an independent nation. Karim Abdian, leader of an Arab-Iranian human rights group, told me federalism could work in Khuzistan if the central government genuinely wants it. "If Arabs can get a fair share of the oil revenues and run their own affairs, then people won't want separation." Speaking of ethnic minorities in general, he added, "If the standard of life is better inside Iran, the minorities won't secede."[36]

U.S. Conservatives Seek to Use Minorities,
but It Won't Be Easy

American conservatives have recently championed the cause of ethnic minorities in Iran. In October 2005 the conservative American Enterprise Institute sponsored a conference with Iranian ethnic minorities, seeking to put the issue into play in Congress and at the White House.

In July 2006 the White House called a meeting of Iranian opposition leaders including ethnic exiles. Attendees included Nicholas Burns, an under secretary of state, and Elliot Abrams, of Iran-Contra fame and a national security advisor in Bush's second term.[37] They didn't take a position on federalism but instead focused on participants' views on Iran's weapons of mass destruction.[38]

Dr. Alireza Nazmi, founder of the South Azerbaijan Diplomatic Commission, attended the White House meeting. "There was a general discussion about minority rights," he told me, "with a lot of yelling and shouting."[39] The exiled leaders couldn't agree among themselves about numerous issues, including federalism and the boundaries of their respective regions.

The United States seeks to use Iran's ethnic minorities to destabilize the Iranian government. Officially, the United States wants to maintain Iran as a single nation. But by sponsoring Kurdish military attacks inside Iran and promoting nationalist groups with questionable backgrounds, the Bush Administration plays a very dangerous game.

During the Cold War, the U.S. government consciously promoted nationalist groups among ethnic minorities in Yugoslavia and the USSR. For years, the Voice of America broadcast the views of separatists and ethnic nationalists as a means to weaken those governments. Officially, the United States wanted to maintain the territorial integrity of those countries, but it helped unleash reactionary nationalist movements with all their ethnic cleansing and war crimes. U.S. leaders don't seem capable of learning from past mistakes.

Stanford's Abbas Milani told me that ethnic minorities certainly have legitimate complaints. "But trying to use that fissure in Iranian society will eventually backfire and consolidate the regime."

NINE

What the U.S. Media Didn't Tell You

After a hard day, reporters working abroad often gather like herds of gazelles at an isolated watering hole. Journalists covering a foreign election, for example, might hang out at a hotel bar to informally exchange information. Iran is no exception—except there are no bars.

During the 2005 presidential elections, I stayed at Tehran's Laleh Hotel along with dozens of other foreign reporters. The coffee shop at the former Intercontinental Hotel substituted for the bar. We got to know one another informally and tended to group together by species: TV reporters, photographers, and print journalists.

It became obvious that American reporters, in particular, had a certain mind-set about Iran. As *Newsweek* reporter Babak Dehghan Pisheh said in another context, "A lot of Western journalists, particularly Americans, come to Iran with a set of stereotypes expecting to see a country more like Saudi Arabia where women aren't allowed to drive. So the stories they write are often very black and white."[1]

Most American reporters I met saw Iran as an evil society and a danger to the United States. While many expressed disagreement with President Bush's policies, they believed Iran was developing a nuclear weapon that threatened America. In short, their views tracked the political consensus emanating from Washington. Rather than proceeding from reality, they filtered their reporting through a Washington lens. When a Washington official makes a statement, even a false one, the major media dutifully report it with few opposing sources.

When those in power lie, accurately reporting their views is not journalism; it's stenography.

Professional reporters from Britain and other European countries attended the same events and interviewed similar sources but came to very different political conclusions. In our book *Target Iraq: What the News Media Didn't Tell You*, Norman Solomon and I described in detail the economic and political reasons why major U.S. media distort reality.[2]

In this chapter, I offer pointed criticisms of mainstream U.S. news coverage of Iran and then suggest some ways you can figure out what's really going on. I focus on the *New York Times* because it's considered the paper of record, and because it plays a key role in shaping other media coverage.

Aircraft Carriers for Peace

At the end of December 2006, Thom Shanker wrote a front-page article in the *New York Times*, detailing the decision to send U.S. aircraft carrier groups to the Persian Gulf. Shanker, paraphrasing unnamed American officers, wrote that the deployment "would be useful in enforcing any sanctions that the United Nations might impose." In addition, he wrote, the ships "entered the Persian Gulf . . . to practice halting vessels suspected of smuggling nuclear materials in waters across the region."[3]

First of all, the UN Security Council had specifically ruled out military force to impose sanctions against Iran, nor were there any prospects of that changing. So the claim that the U.S. Navy entered the Gulf to help the UN was clearly wrong. Secondly, neither Shanker nor anyone else offered credible evidence that Iran plans to smuggle nuclear materials by sea. The *Times* relied solely on U.S. and British military officials. Shanker didn't even pretend to offer balance by quoting Iranian officials or anyone else critical of U.S. policy.

The article assumed Iran was a threat to the American people and the United States was responding defensively. In reality, the United States sent an armada to the Persian Gulf to pressure Iran and prepare for possible unilateral military action.

That kind of one-sided story most often appears with a Washington dateline, where top leaders cultivate reporters who aspire to become chief stenographer. The Lewis "Scooter" Libby perjury trial in February 2007 laid bare the incestuous relations between top officials and major media figures.

Vice President Dick Cheney's Chief of Staff Libby and presidential advisor Karl Rove called selected journalists, such as Judith Miller of the *New York Times* and Matt Cooper of *Time* magazine, to plant stories discrediting a whistle blower who told the truth about the nonexistent nuclear weapons program in Iraq. As a result, Valerie Plame was exposed as a CIA officer and eventually had to leave her job.

While Washington reporters are the worst offenders, reporters in the field can accept the most preposterous stories as well, so long as they come from official American sources.

On January 20, 2007, men dressed as U.S. soldiers and carrying U.S. identification cards attacked a meeting of Iraqi and American soldiers in the city of Karbala, Iraq. Five Americans eventually died as a result of the assault, which took the United States completely by surprise and constituted a huge embarrassment. A few days later, Iraqi and American military investigators floated the story that Iranians may have prepared the attack. CNN quoted unnamed "officials" as saying, "This was beyond what we have seen militias or foreign fighters do."[4]

The officials presented no physical evidence or other proof of Iranian involvement, just conspiracy theories. The allegation dovetailed nicely with the U.S. campaign to demonize Iran for killing American soldiers in Iraq. It appeared far more likely that senior Iraqi officials were involved, because the attackers knew the exact time and location of the high-level meeting. After an initial flurry of speculative stories alleging Iranian involvement, the story just died out because of a lack of any credible evidence.

These examples are more than aberrations. A careful reading of major U.S. media shows a particular bias, one so strong that reporters don't even see it.

The Assumptions of Empire

To put the U.S. media coverage in perspective, imagine for a moment that we're living in Britain in 1946. Politicians, military leaders, business tycoons, and the media all agree that Britain has a splendid empire. We have just won a world war.

We have brought prosperity, culture, and Christianity to natives throughout the world. True, the locals periodically complain or even riot. (There *is* that pesky Gandhi fellow.) But certainly no one would suggest that we grant them independence. What an absurd idea!

Within fifteen years, anti-imperialist movements forced the collapse of that very splendid empire. But don't look to the mainstream British media to have hinted at that possibility until the empire had already begun to crack. More typically, they provided distorted news about the anticolonial movements by quoting only official British sources.

For example, the BBC reported that widespread "riots" had broken out on the British Crown Colony of Cyprus in 1956. "Archbishop Makarios, the leader of the 'enosis' campaign to unify Cyprus with Greece, was arrested for 'actively fostering terrorism' and has been deported to the Seychelles. British security forces have searched the archbishop's residence and say they have found one petrol bomb and ten similar bombs."[5]

In reality, the people of Cyprus were rebelling against colonial rule. The demonstrations continued and by 1960 Cyprus had won independence. Archbishop Makarios was elected president, proving once again that yesterday's terrorist is today's statesman.

Today, the U.S. empire dwarfs that of its British precursor. America is the only superpower. The United States has the largest military in world history, with over 737 military bases around the world.[6] And like their Fleet Street counterparts of old, today's U.S. media defend the empire. News coverage might agree or disagree about a particular policy, roughly reflecting the differences between high-ranking Republicans and Democrats. Some reporters might question the country's leadership when policies go very poorly. But few question the underlying assumptions of empire.

The Corporate Owners Call the Shots

The content of the media reflects the interests of their corporate owners. These days, six companies own the large majority of news and entertainment media in the United States: Time Warner (CNN), Disney (ABC), Murdoch's News Corporation (Fox), Bertelsmann of Germany (Doubleday publishing), Viacom (CBS), and General Electric (NBC).[7]

These companies have vested corporate interests to protect. None wants to see critical stories about its own holdings, which in some cases include war industries. And corporate executives certainly don't want to alienate government officials who handle antitrust matters, renew Federal Communications Commission licenses, and offer lucrative government contracts. No one wants to be seen as undercutting national security by publishing embarrassing articles.

In subtle and not so subtle ways, owners make clear their media enterprises should avoid certain topics. If writing critical stories, reporters must keep the stability of the empire in mind. Editors and reporters who have survived on the job usually internalize those lessons.

In theory, major media don't allow government officials to censor the news. But when the story is sensitive enough, editors check with top government officials prior to publication, using the argument that the editors want to protect national security. On several occasions, top editors at the *New York Times* admitted to delaying publication and changing the content of important investigative stories—in part, because government officials objected.

In December 2005 the *New York Times* published an expose of how the National Security Agency wiretapped American phone calls without warrants. It had held up the story
since before the November 2004 elections—in effect, allowing the administration to censor the newspaper's content. A
similar process took place during the editing of a 2006 story
about improper U.S. pressure on European banks to track alleged terrorists.[8]

That process of corporate and government pressure certainly applies to mainstream coverage of Iran.

Iran's Activities in Iraq—a Case Study

In December 2006, the Bush Administration launched a propaganda blitz to blame Iran for killing American soldiers in
Iraq. In press briefings and speeches, the United States alleged
that Iran was supplying mortars, rocket-propelled grenades,
and other small arms to certain Iraqi militia groups targeting
Americans. The Iranian government was allegedly manufac-
turing highly sophisticated explosively formed penetrators
(EFPs) to blow up armored Humvees.

In the beginning, the major media dutifully and uncritically reported those assertions. CBS *Evening News* anchor
Katie Couric said, "The U.S. military says it has proof positive" of Iranian weapons in Iran.[9] *New York Times* reporter
Michael Gordon, who had coauthored false stories about
Saddam's weapons of mass destruction back in 2003, also promoted the Pentagon's views about the new crisis. Writing
from Washington, Gordon quoted U.S. military sources alleging that top Iranian leaders, including Supreme Leader Khamenei, were responsible for providing EFPs to Iraqi militias.[10]

In February 2006 the military held a Baghdad briefing for

reporters, in which unnamed officials presented a table over-flowing with weapons allegedly made in Iran. They claimed similar weapons killed 170 American soldiers over the previous three years. To their credit, some U.S. reporters questioned parts of the presentation. James Glanz in the *New York Times* asked why the briefers insisted on anonymity and how they could prove high Iranian officials were responsible. He also asked in his story if the information was being presented now to justify war with Iran. By the low standards set during the 2003 run up to the Iraq invasion, these questions constituted fiery dissent from administration propaganda.

But most American reporters accepted the underlying premise of the military presentation. Glanz wrote, "Whatever doubts were created about the timing and circumstances of the weapons disclosures, the direct physical evidence presented on Sunday was extraordinary."[11]

That became the framework for much of the coverage in other U.S. media: Iran is providing deadly munitions to Iraqi militias, but the administration hasn't proven top leaders had approved. That angle on the story got repeated in countless other media throughout the United States.

In the weeks after the original February 11, 2007, press briefing, some articles in the *Times* and other major media became more skeptical about whether the EFPs could have originated only in Iran. But none of them accurately described the phony intelligence as well as the same-day reporting by some of the British and alternative press.

Criticizing Conventional Wisdom in Real Time

As someone who writes for mainstream dailies and broadcast networks, I know how hard it is to file a story the day of a bombshell U.S. announcement. Every other journalist around you will report the official version of events, perhaps with some caveats. Your editor doesn't want to run something different and risk attack by the administration and its supporters.

But it is possible to scrutinize the conventional wisdom in real time. That's what some of the British media did. Public opinion in Britain overwhelmingly opposes the occupation of Iraq and any military assault on Iran. So the British media have greater political space to write contrary—and truthful—stories. Accurate journalism, in turn, increases public sentiment against war with Iran.

On the same day that the *New York Times* reported the "extraordinary" evidence, London's *Independent* newspaper ran a front-page article that said, in its second paragraph, "The allegations against Iran are similar in tone and credibility to those made four years ago by the U.S. government about Iraq possessing weapons of mass destruction in order to justify the invasion of 2003."[12]

Paul Reynolds, a BBC world affairs correspondent, dug through old articles and official statements to come up with one of the first articles to question the underlying premise of the U.S. military propaganda. He noted that British army officers no longer claimed that Iran makes the EFPs. Reynolds wrote that British officers say that "the technology matched bomb-making found elsewhere in the Middle East, including Lebanon and Syria."[13] Reynolds wrote that, contrary to U.S. military reports, the manufacture of EFPs does not require sophisticated equipment. He pointed out that "Iraqis themselves would be capable of copying a design and therefore do not need to get bombs from Iran."

Several weeks prior to the Baghdad press briefing, the *Los Angeles Times* ran an excellent article pointing out that U.S.

troops in the field had found little evidence of Iranian munitions being used against them.[14]

Plenty of alternative media in the United States wrote stories showing that Iran played no significant military role in
the deaths of American soldiers.[15] Some politicians in the future will probably claim that they were fooled by the Bush
Administration lies about Iran. But those lies were exposed
publicly within days of the press briefing. And you didn't
need access to classified documents to figure out the Bush
plans. You just had to take off the blinders provided by the
empire builders.

A Fair Response

I contacted *New York Times* reporters criticized in this chapter, but none gave substantive responses to my e-mails. *Times*
Public Editor Byron Calame did respond publicly in his column to readers' criticism of Iran coverage.[16] He gave the
Times a clean bill of health!

Calame even praised Michael Gordon's incredibly one-
sided and downright inaccurate story of February 10, 2006. In
a piece of legerdemain conducted best by the *Times*, Calame
praised Gordon for seeking out dissenting views. The Gordon
article, he wrote, "cited interviews with 'civilian and military
officials from a broad range of government agencies,' and
pointed out that group included 'some whose agencies have
previously been skeptical about the significance of Iran's role
in Iraq.'"

And so we have the perfect defense of empire. The *Times*
remains balanced so long as it seeks out dissenting views
within the government. The *Times* has no need to find

sources outside the Washington beltway or those who oppose intervention in Iran altogether.

Calame did raise one criticism of Gordon's work. Since June 2005, the *Times* decided to explain to readers why a given source must remain anonymous.[17] Public Editor Calame chastised Michael Gordon for not mentioning why his sources requested anonymity, but not for using them in the first place.

Controlling the News

I've filed stories from around the world. By far the worst cities for doing good journalism in the Western world are Washington DC and Los Angeles. They are both home to powerful elites who want to control the news. In Los Angeles, the power mongers of the entertainment industry manipulate the media to create favorable coverage and retaliate against reporters who don't play ball. The top political, business, and military leaders of Washington play the same game. But the stakes are much higher.

Just for starters, most government officials won't talk to reporters on the record. We can quote them but not use their names. That's why papers are filled with so many anonymous sources. By refusing to be quoted by name, bureaucrats can avoid responsibility for their statements, and journalists lose credibility with the public.

I tried to interview middle-level State Department officials for this book, but by official policy, they wouldn't speak on the record. So I asked to meet with people who could use their names. No one agreed. I even tried to interview a person at Freedom House, a major centrist human rights group, but she wouldn't talk on the record. Giving anonymous quotes has become the norm, not the exception, in Washington. Apparently, media manipulation is contagious.

Reporters quickly learn to play the Washington game. If you write stories favorable to your sources, you get interviews with higher-ups. If you don't interview powerful people, the editors notice, and you're weeded out. Young reporters spend years waiting for plum jobs covering the State Department, Pentagon, or White House. Those beats have lots of prestige and six-figure salaries. Sometimes they are gateways to higher positions in the media; other times they lead directly to jobs in politics or with corporations.

I have seen many young reporters work their way up through the mainstream press. They like the increased pay and prestige that comes with writing for a major daily or big network. But the pressure to conform is intense. You learn quickly not to cause waves.

Former National Public Radio correspondent Sara Chayes wrote about her experiences reporting from abroad. "When in doubt, you conform. It is the safest course, and it is the course your editors feel comfortable with. That stuff about scoops was never my experience. . . . My editors . . . never liked having me out on a limb."[18]

So for those conservatives who believe that liberals have conspired to control the major media and destroy America, take heart! Yes, more reporters register Democrat than Republican. But most shed their personal views on the job like a snake in the desert sun. The long crawl to the top changes their thinking, and their desire to keep the cushy job keeps them aligned with whoever is in power.

And don't forget the economic factors. Newspapers, radio, and TV networks are generally profitable in the United States—but not profitable enough for their corporate owners.

For example, the *Los Angeles Times* has earned 20 percent profit, roughly twice what a typical Fortune 500 company makes. Yet Wall Street insists that newspapers will lose profits in the future, so they must earn more than 20 percent now.[19]

Each year we see a wave of mergers, takeovers, and corporate dismemberments. Companies take on debt and then lay off reporters and editors. They close foreign and domestic bureaus. Reporters at formerly stable media companies suddenly fear losing their jobs. The prospect of imminent unemployment isn't conducive to taking risks.

So it's easier for journalists to keep their heads down and report the same things as everyone else. But occasionally they don't. And that's when the story gets really interesting.

The Journalistic High Jump

Occasionally, courageous reporters come up with important stories that shatter the conventional wisdom. In 2003, Carlotta Gall, a *New York Times* reporter based in Kabul, dug out a story of how the U.S. military tortured and killed two prisoners at Bagram air base in Afghanistan.[20] She even found the prisoners' official death certificates indicating homicide, signed by an American pathologist. The story sat unpublished for weeks. Editors sent her out to do more reporting.

That's what editors do with stories challenging conventional Washington wisdom. An editor can always demand more reporting, raising the journalistic bar to impossible heights. By contrast, stories reflecting the Washington consensus can be published with the bar at knee level.

Doug Frantz, who was the *New York Times* investigative editor, revealed to the *Columbia Journalism Review* some of the internal *Times* discussions about Gall's article. Top editor

Howell Raines and others, according to Frantz, insisted that the torture story "was improbable; it was hard to get their mind around. . . . Compare Judy Miller's WMD stories to Carlotta's story. On a scale of one to ten, Carlotta's story was nailed down to ten."[21] Finally, after sitting for a month, the story ran on page 14, not on page 1 as originally pushed by her editor. It ran just a few weeks prior to the U.S. invasion of Iraq and had little public impact.

Washington Post reporter Dana Priest faced a different kind of problem. Priest has written some excellent articles exposing U.S. prisoner abuse and the "extraordinary rendition" (i.e., kidnapping) of alleged terrorists to other countries for torture. In late 2005, Priest published a front-page article about the CIA's secret prisons.[22] The article hit a nerve in Washington because the war in Iraq was becoming increasingly unpopular and European media were exposing the CIA activities.

Instead of moving to stop the illegal and immoral CIA kidnappings, official Washington reacted by threatening to prosecute those who leaked information to the *Post*. The Justice Department and House Intelligence Committee launched probes into the leaks—but ignored the U.S. policy of torture and kidnapping.

But such articles are the rare exception. The administration in power usually gets full cooperation in efforts to demonize the enemy du jour.[23] And in the last few years, that process has gotten some new media cheerleaders.

Bring in the Clowns

So far I have intentionally not mentioned media distortions from Fox News and other outlets with obvious right-wing bias. Fox pioneered the intentional blurring of the line between reporting and commentary. It set up programs that looked like news shows but featured right-wing blowhards spouting unsubstantiated opinion. MSNBC and CNN followed suit in an effort to grab ratings and advertisers.

The cable TV networks thrive on sensationalistic stories about rampaging serial killers or astronauts attempting to kidnap their lovers' girlfriends.[24] But Iran also provides perfect fodder because the United States can be presented as the good guy going after evil mullah extremists.

Earlier in this chapter I described the journalistic high-jump bar required to air a particular story. In the case of Fox News, they just throw the bar to the sidelines. *Fox and Friends* cohost Steve Doocy once reported Iran was only sixteen *days* away from building a nuclear bomb, citing an unnamed source at the U.S. Embassy in Moscow. That preposterous story was quickly dropped.[25]

In 2006, CNN hired Glenn Beck, a right-wing radio talk-show zealot and self-described rodeo clown, to host an evening prime-time program. While Beck admits he is not a journalist, he presents video clips of the day's events, interviews guests, and otherwise appears to be one. He regularly exaggerates the threat that Iran presents to the United States, referring to President Ahmadinejad as "President Tom."

Beck said on one program, "In 1938 it took Hitler roughly six months to march across Europe after Chamberlain's big 'peace in our time' moment. How much longer do we have with President Tom? Six months, twelve months?"[26]

Beck once interviewed Keith Ellison, a moderate Muslim elected to the House of Representatives. Beck revealed a deep-seated anti-Muslim bias by somehow equating an African

American Muslim with terrorists. Beck said, "I have been nervous about this interview with you because what I feel like saying is, 'Sir, prove to me that you are not working with our enemies.'"[27]

Such claptrap would be laughable, except some people take it seriously. In actual numbers, conservative cable TV reaches relatively few people. The top Fox News broadcast reaches just under 1.5 million viewers a night, compared to over 9 million for ABC television's evening news. All together, the major cable news channels reach just under 2.5 million, while the three major networks have about 25 million viewers.[28] But because the right-wingers are favored by sectors of the ruling elite, they have a political impact beyond their limited audience. Cable channels play up conservative views, which get echoed on conservative talk radio and in right-wing blogs. Pretty soon, the most outrageous charges begin to sound legitimate.

Decoding the Media

OK, the right-wing and mainstream media have the uncomfortable habit of lying. How do I figure out what's going on? Glad you asked.

If you want to find the location of a radio transmitter, you get a fix on its signal from two other directions. The process is called triangulation. You can use a similar method to triangulate the truth from the media.

I read three newspapers a day (*San Francisco Chronicle*, *New York Times*, and *Wall Street Journal*). I watch broadcast TV and listen to public radio. I regularly read alternative newspapers, magazines, and Web sites. On important stories,

I might consult British media (*BBC*, the *Guardian*, the *Independent*), Al Jazeera English language service, or various newspapers from Europe and Latin America.

I don't expect the average reader to devote that much time to the media. But by understanding mainstream media biases and adding alternative information, you can figure out what's going on. Here are some handy hints.

• *Watch for the dateline.* Washington politicians love to cultivate reporters favorable to their causes. So the administration in power starts its propaganda blitzes with reporters high up in the Washington food chain. Anything datelined Washington should be read with particular scrutiny. Beat reporters at the Pentagon, for example, rely on current and former military officers as sources. (I've yet to meet a beat reporter for the peace movement.) By looking carefully at the sources, you can usually figure out who initiated the story: someone in power (usually), or someone going after those in power (very rarely).

The Washington dateline can be helpful when one section of the ruling elite wants to attack another. Sometimes Washington reporters break very interesting stories about disagreements between the Defense and State departments, for example. In the run up to the Iraq war, some intelligence and diplomatic officials leaked stories undercutting the Bush Administration's arguments for invading Iraq. But just because one sector of the ruling elite disagrees with the other, that doesn't necessarily mean either one is right.

• *Scrutinize the sources.* Always be suspicious of articles that describe events in foreign countries with sources based only in the United States. Some mainstream journalists reporting from abroad have the uncomfortable habit of phoning back to the United States to find so-called experts to explain policy issues. If they can't find an expert inside the country, you should be suspicious.

• *Look carefully at the so-called experts.* Are they former government or corporate officials? Major media almost always use experts who reflect the policy debate between top-level Democrats and Republicans or between various branches of government. If the story doesn't quote sources genuinely critical of the new policy being advocated, for example, find some additional sources on the Internet.

• *Get to know the bylines.* Some reporters report more honestly than others. Some are shills for the ruling elite. I don't agree with everything that they write, but I respect the reporting of *Times* reporters such as Carlotta Gall, Stephen Kinzer, and recently retired Chris Hedges. *Washington Post* reporters Dana Priest and Dafna Linzer have written excellent stories. The *New Yorker*'s Seymour Hersh stands in a class of his own for digging out contrary views among intelligence officials.

As a media consumer, you might get angry at a particular article and fire off a letter to the editor. But if you see a particularly good article, you should also send a letter or e-mail of support. Good reporters are like Maytag repairmen; they can get pretty lonely.

• *Read the foreign press and alternative media.* As a college student at the University of California, Berkeley, in the 1960s, I had to wait five days for European newspapers to arrive at Dave's Smoke Shop, and months longer for more esoteric journals. Today such information is available online in real time. But more is not always better. Learn to distinguish between Web sites that offer unsubstantiated rumors and those with hard facts, between those promoting conspiracy theories and those offering a sharp critique of the empire. Would you believe everything contained in a leaflet handed out on the street? Take the same attitude toward the Internet.

As with all media, keep in mind the biases of the particular Internet site. I don't trust the BBC's coverage of northern Ireland, for example, because it hews too closely to the British government's viewpoint. The BBC and the *Guardian*, on the other hand, often provide good coverage of Iran and the Middle East. Some of my other favorites include www.Truth Dig.com, www.TruthOut.org, www.commondreams.org, and www.Alternet.com.

The mainstream media has reflected Washington's perspective on Iran: Iran not only threatens to develop nuclear weapons and backs terrorists, it's murdering American soldiers in Iraq. All options must remain on the table. The rhetoric coming out of Washington and duly reported in the media has an eerie familiarity. So it's appropriate in the final chapter to look at some lessons from the Iraq war.

TEN

Learning the Lessons of Iraq

In the months leading up to the U.S. invasion of Iraq in March 2003, I spoke at dozens of community centers, churches, and campuses across the country. I argued that Saddam Hussein had no weapons of mass destruction and that he posed no immediate threat to the people of the United States. A U.S. occupation of Iraq could lead to splintering the country to the benefit of Iran.[1]

But I still remember a question from a young college student in southern Oregon. "What if Saddam Hussein gives nuclear weapons to terrorists, and they attack the United States?" she asked. "Isn't it worth the risk of war to stop such devastation?" I responded by saying that Saddam didn't have ties with Al Qaeda and that what she described was an administration myth.

I don't know what impact my response had on the young woman. I was responding with rational argument while Bush was appealing to the gut. Many Americans supported the Iraq war in the early years, fearing that if we didn't stop the terrorists in Iraq, we would have to stop them in America.

By 2006 the United States had engaged in the same kind of propaganda campaign against Iran. But in order to understand it, we must look at the real lessons of the Iraq war.

No Cakewalk in Iraq

A small group of neoconservative Republicans had hoped to invade Iraq for years. This was a group of fiercely right-wing intellectuals, some of whom had once considered themselves leftists. They took a hard line against communism and later against Islamic countries. In 1998 the neoconservative group Project for the New American Century wrote a position paper calling for the overthrow of Saddam Hussein. The project included such future luminaries as Vice President Dick Cheney, Secretary of Defense Donald Rumsfeld, and Deputy Secretary of Defense Paul Wolfowitz.

The neoconservatives advocated that nut-brain policy, which had few adherents until the atrocity of September 11, 2001. They tried to blame the 9/11 attacks on Iraq but didn't have any evidence. So they bided their time.

In the fall of 2002, the Bush Administration thought it had won in Afghanistan and had strong support from the American people. It cooked up intelligence that Iraq possessed chemical and biological weapons, had restarted its nuclear weapons program, and was supporting Al Qaeda. In fact, the United States invaded Iraq for the same reason it threatened Iran: hegemonic control of the Middle East.[2] Even former National Security Advisor Zbigniew Brzezinski, a Democratic hawk, said many people in the Middle East fear a "new and enduring American imperial hegemony" in the region.[3]

Many politicians criticized the Bush Administration for having no plan for the Iraq occupation. In fact, the administration did have a plan. The people of Iraq just didn't cooperate. The United States would gain quick military victory over Saddam Hussein, and residents would greet U.S. troops as liberators, throwing flowers and candy. The United States would remove the country's top leaders but maintain the army, police, and civilian bureaucracy. A pro-U.S. strongman would emerge as Iraq's leader.

The United States would privatize Iraq's oil industry to pay for the occupation. Once Iraq became stable, the United States could effect regime change in Iran, Syria, and Lebanon and force the Palestinians to accept whatever deal the Israelis offered. The government has declassified documents that show American official plans were truly out of touch with reality. The plan called for the reduction of U.S. troops in Iraq to 5,000 within thirty-two to forty-five months of the war's start.[4]

Of course, the plan was fatally flawed. The Iraqi people welcomed the overthrow of Saddam, but never wanted U.S. domination. The army had largely disintegrated even before the U.S. authorities formally dissolved it. Iranian-backed Shiite political parties gained the most votes in elections. The U.S.-backed strongman Iyad Allawi lost the election and went into self-imposed exile in London. Ahmad Chalabi, the on-again-off-again U.S. ally, couldn't even get elected to parliament.

Without an effective central government, opportunistic political leaders used ethnic and religious divisions to build up their own power. In February 2006, right-wing Sunni extremists bombed the holy Shiite shrine in Samara, setting off a full-scale civil war between Sunnis and Shiites. While certainly differences had existed during Saddam's rule, the two communities had lived side by side without violence.

Incredibly, the Bush Administration, and the neoconservatives in particular, think the basic plan for Iraq has proven correct. Former U.S. ambassador to Saudi Arabia Charles Freeman, Jr., told me, "The neoconservative group think their good ideas were poorly implemented in Iraq."[5]

Then the neoconservatives offered the same skewed analysis of Iran. They argued that the Iranian government is unpopular with its own people and only needs a shove from the United States for the people to rise up. Michael Ledeen, a leading neoconservative at the American Enterprise Institute, wrote that "there is good reason to believe the country is ripe for a pro-Western democratic revolution."[6]

Freeman said the neocon argument is extremely moralistic. "If you're an inherently good power like the United States," he said, "you must use your power to make sure good, justice, and the American way prevail over evil. Somehow there will be an uprising in Iran." He summarized the neocon lesson of the Iraq war: "If at first you don't succeed, do the same thing again somewhere else."

Starting in the fall of 2006, the United States began a concerted campaign to blame Iran for U.S. casualties in Iraq as both a diplomatic pressure tactic and a prelude to possible military strikes against Iran. The clerical government does have strong ties to Iraq, but is Iran a threat to American troops as claimed?

Iran's Influence in Iraq

Just outside Tehran's old bazaar, dozens of vendors and store owners have set up shop. During the Iran-Iraq war, an estimated six hundred thousand Shiite Iraqis were expelled or fled to Iran. Merchants established small stores in this neighborhood as a way to survive during years of exile. My inter-

preter and I wandered into a variety of stores and were welcomed with cups of tea and nut-filled pastries.

We found a hole-in-the-wall shop selling beads. We
squeezed inside and heard the owner's tales of abuse and torture at the hands of Saddam Hussein's regime. Many Iraqi
exiles welcomed the 2003 U.S. invasion as a means to rid their
country of dictatorship. Zuhair Razavi, the bead shop owner,
told me Iraqis "kiss the hands of the Americans" in thanks for
overthrowing Saddam. He now thinks it's time for Iraq to establish an Islamic state.[7]

That lays bare the contradiction of U.S. policy. Iran had
close ties with the two Kurdish and three Shiite political parties that made up the majority of Iraq's ruling coalition.
Shiites are the majority in Iraq, and Iran always planned to
play an influential role in whatever government emerged.

Leaders of the moderate Islamist Dawa Party lived in Iran
for years. The Supreme Council for the Islamic Revolution in
Iraq (SCIRI), with its armed Badr Brigades militia, was
founded in Iran. One day, I decided to interview the SCIRI
spokesperson in Iran.

I took a taxi to a prosperous section of Tehran full of commercial buildings. SCIRI occupies a large, four-story office
building, which sources told me is paid for by the Iranian government. Before the 2003 fall of Saddam, two hundred people
worked here, but most have now returned to Iraq. SCIRI
received the second-highest number of seats in the 2005
elections.

"Iran and Iraq have a very, very good relationship," Majid
Ghammas, head of SCIRI in Iran, told me. "The Iranian government understood the situation in Iraq better than other
countries."[8] SCIRI favors a politically fundamentalist inter-

pretation of Islam. "Iraq should be an Islamic state," said Ghammas. "Islam should be the source for our constitution, and no law should be approved that is against Islam."

Iran Covers All the Bases

Iranian leaders are quite pragmatic, having supported SCIRI and Dawa. They also supported Muqtada al-Sadr, a fiery Muslim cleric who at times fought Americans and at other times participated in electoral politics as a key part of the ruling coalition. For years, Iran threw support behind Kurdish leader Jalal Talabani, who is now president of Iraq.

"We think America has done the best work for us, removing Saddam, our worst enemy," Mehdi Rafsanjani told me. He is the son of former president Ali Akbar Hashemi Rafsanjani and was a campaign manager for his father's 2005 presidential campaign. "Anyone who comes to power in Iraq, it's no problem. These are all our friends."[9]

Asked if it's ironic that when the United States eventually withdraws, Iran could have greater influence than the United States, Hamid-Reza Asefi, deputy foreign minister under President Khatami, told me, "That is true. But that's not our fault. When Americans are working for us, we'll let them do it."[10]

The United States accused Iran of not only giving political and economic support but also providing critical munitions to groups attacking U.S. soldiers in Iraq. Philip Zelikow, Counselor of the Department of State from 2005 to 2006, told me that since 2005, "Iran was very actively involved in assisting insurgents and gangs inside Iraq in killing Americans and in killing British soldiers and civilians as well."[11] He wouldn't specify which particular insurgent groups.

Iran certainly isn't supporting Al Qaeda or other fundamentalist Sunnis in Iraq. In fact, the Iraqi branch of Al Qaeda wants Iran destroyed. Abu-Umar al-Husayni al-Qurayshi al-Baghdadi, the leader of Al Qaeda in Iraq, encouraged the United States to drop a nuclear bomb on Iran. "Our battle with the Persians has started," he said in a 2007 audio statement monitored by U.S. intelligence.[12]

Iran benefits from having Shiite Muslim allies in power, not Sunnis. Iranian sources admitted to me that they send arms to the Shiite Muslim militias, but they argued that aid is intended to fight the insurgents, not kill Americans. Remember, they said, United States is arming the same militias under the guise of building up the Iraqi army.

Officially, the Iranian government called for establishing a timetable for withdrawal of U.S. troops from Iraq. But in reality, the Iranians wanted the United States to stay for the medium term. Diplomats familiar with Iranian policy told me Iran's allied parties aren't strong enough to fight the guerrillas on their own. Iran hoped that the United States could crush the insurgency, and then free elections would maintain their allies in power. If Iraq eventually breaks apart into Kurdish, Sunni, and Shiite countries, then Iranian officials think they will have strong influence in Kurdistan and the Shia state. In either eventuality, it makes no sense for Iran to sponsor attacks on American troops, they said.

Military Attack?

A sector of the American ruling elite strongly advocated military strikes against Iran that they hoped would topple the government. They didn't envision an invasion and occupation. Rather, aerial bombing would lead to a popular uprising and regime change. That's the real goal, not deterring Iran's nuclear threat or stopping the death of American troops in Iraq.

Thomas McInerney, a retired Air Force lieutenant general and military analyst for Fox News, wrote, "If we were to carry out an air campaign, it would probably unleash a new Iranian revolution. . . . We could use the Afghan model of precision airpower supporting covert and indigenous forces."[13]

Seymour Hersh reported as far back as spring of 2006 that, in the words of one former defense official, the Bush Administration was considering a "sustained bombing campaign, . . . [which would] humiliate the religious leadership and lead the public to rise up and overthrow the government. I was shocked when I heard it, and asked myself 'what are they smoking?'"[14]

To politically isolate Iran, the Bush Administration began to fan up anti-Shiite fears among Sunni Muslims throughout the region. The Bush Administration suspected Shiites in the small Gulf state of Bahrain would support Iran in a future confrontation with the United States. Bahrain is about 70 percent Shiite but is ruled by a Sunni royal family. So right-wing Sunnis launched a vicious campaign accusing the local Shiite community of being Iranian agents.[15]

The United States also encouraged Saudi Arabia to fund right-wing Sunni terrorist groups in Lebanon. Ironically, this new strategy of allying with conservative Sunnis against Shiite Iran put the United States in bed with political movements sympathetic to Al Qaeda.[16] The United States promoted a similar alliance in the 1980s with fundamentalist Sunnis to fight the Soviet occupation of Afghanistan. Some guerrillas and others who worked with the United States, such as Osama bin Laden, ended up forming Al Qaeda.

Israel's ruling elite also strongly supported an attack on Iran. Former Israeli prime minister Benjamin Netanyahu argued that Iran poses an immediate and mortal threat to Israel.[17] Israeli military authorities leaked information to the British press that they had active contingency plans to bomb Iran's nuclear facilities with atomic weapons.[18]

But Israel won't initiate an attack on Iran without explicit approval from the United States. Logistically, Israeli planes would have to fly over Iraq, which would require U.S. permission. Politically, the United States loses credibility with Sunni Arab countries if it allows Israel to attack. The United States prevented Israel from attacking Iraq during the 1991 Gulf War, although Saddam Hussein was raining rockets onto Israel. Israel's direct involvement would have shattered the U.S. alliance with Arab countries such as Saudi Arabia and Syria.

Significantly, not a single major ally except Israel supported U.S. military action against Iran. Even Britain's Prime Minister Tony Blair spoke out publicly against U.S. military strikes.[19] During the invasion of Iraq, the United States bribed and cajoled a paltry group of countries into what it called the "Coalition of the Willing." If the USA attacks Iran, it will spearhead the "Coalition of the Nonexistent."

The United States certainly has the military capability of dropping bombs and launching missiles against Iran with few or no American casualties. Initially, the public and some Democratic Party leaders would likely rally round the president for acting tough against the Iranian threat. But what would happen after the first few days and weeks?

The Results of a U.S. Attack

To explore that question, Colonel Sam Gardiner (U.S. Air Force, retired) conducted a mock war games exercise for the *Atlantic Monthly* magazine.[20] The war games revealed a number of critical military and political problems. The United States can't be sure exactly where Iran's nuclear facilities are located and how well they are protected. So massive and repeated strikes may be necessary. Many Iranian civilians could be killed. If the bombings release radioactive materials, they may drift over civilian areas and even into neighboring countries. The Iranian public will likely rally around its leadership in the face of a horrific external attack.

Iran will respond militarily, although not necessarily with a conventional attack on U.S. ships or bases. "There's no doubt in my mind that this would be an act of war," former CIA intelligence officer Paul Pillar told me. "There would be Iranian retaliation."[21]

Iran could close the Strait of Hormuz, through which 25 percent of the world's oil supplies pass. Even the threat of such a closing would send oil prices skyrocketing. Iran could encourage Hizbollah to launch missiles into Israel. Any U.S. attack against Iran would outrage Muslims, igniting large demonstrations in Europe, the Middle East, and Asia. Iran could mobilize that anger and encourage Shiite parties in Iraq to attack U.S. troops.

Finally, in a truly nightmare scenario, Iran could encourage terrorist attacks inside the United States and in allied countries. When I interviewed Syria's President Bashar al-Asad in 2006, he said, "If you do a military strike, you will have chaos. It's very dangerous."[22]

When I visited Washington DC in early 2007, I tried to

find any Bush Administration supporter who could spell out what military victory would look like in Iran, beyond vague promises of a popular uprising. I couldn't find any.

Pillar told me that's because the administration is repeating the same errors it made in Iraq. "I fear it hasn't been thought out and gamed out, even though it should be," he said. "Instead, it gets reduced to the 1 percent solution idea. Focusing on one particular threat, the Iranian Bomb and worst-case scenario, that's so bad we have to do something about it regardless."

In the most chilling interview of my Washington trip, Pillar calmly said, "I believe there is a significant chance that this administration, before it leaves office in January '09, will attempt a military strike against Iran. I hope that doesn't happen. My personal view is that would be a major blunder. The consequences of Iranian retaliation against U.S. interests . . . in the region and worldwide would be severe."

And that's from the CIA guy who was in charge of Iranian intelligence during the first administration of George W. Bush.

Luckily, not everyone in power favors the military option.

Not Just Republicans versus Democrats

One afternoon I drove down to the Hoover Institution at Stanford University. The Hoover Tower looms over the idyllic campus, a conservative fortress in an otherwise liberal village. The immediate problem, however, was parking. There wasn't any. After wandering around various parking lots and idling in front of people not inclined to leave their precious parking spaces, I found a metered spot. I trudged over to meet Abbas Milani at an office building for Hoover fellows.

A gaggle of Army officers had gathered in the lobby. They were consulting with some of the Hoover fellows, just another day in an institution stuffed with former cabinet members and assorted conservatives. Abbas Milani, an academic and former leftist, doesn't fit the typical Hoover mold. But he's become known as one of the country's top Iran experts.

In April 2006, President Bush met with Milani at the Hoover Institution. "I was very pleasantly surprised at how involved he was with the Iran issue," Milani told me. Far from his image as an inarticulate doofus, Bush asked intelligent questions about the different political tendencies within Iran's ruling class. "He knew the factions. He knew their names. This notion of him as someone who knows nothing about the world was simply not my experience."[23]

Milani explained that based on his conversations with officials, two camps exist within the Bush Administration. One advocates military strikes against Iran as soon as possible. Vice President Cheney heads this group. "They think the regime is incorrigible and the only way is to take them out," said Milani.

Another camp within the administration, which includes Secretary of State Condoleezza Rice, favors other forms of pressure. "They don't think Iran is an easy target. They want to see if they can work with the European Union, and with Russia and China, to bring economic pressure to get the Islamic regime off the nuclear track."

Milani and other experts say neither camp is prepared to live with a clerical government in power in Iran; they differ mainly on the tactics to remove it. "Both sides ultimately think that this regime is up to no good," said Milani. "The only long-term way the United States can coexist with them is if there is regime change."

Those two camps exist within the Democratic Party, as well. When the Clinton Administration was in power, it didn't threaten to attack Iran militarily, but it did pressure Iran economically by championing the Iran-Libya Sanctions Act. In the run-up to the 2008 elections, leading Democratic contenders for president took tough stands on Iran, including advocacy of possible military action.

Senator Hilary Clinton, Democrat from New York, said, "We cannot, we should not, we must not permit Iran to build or acquire nuclear weapons. In dealing with this threat, . . . no option can be taken off the table."[24]

John Edwards, 2004 Democratic vice-presidential candidate, told the attendees of a major Israeli security conference, "To ensure that Iran never gets nuclear weapons, we need to keep all options on the table. Let me reiterate—all options."[25]

Representative Nancy Pelosi, a liberal Democrat from San Francisco who was elected speaker of the house in 2007, takes a hawkish line on Middle East issues affecting Israel. She told a meeting of the American Israel Public Affairs Committee, "The greatest threat to Israel's right to exist, with the prospect of devastating violence, now comes from Iran."[26]

A few Democratic politicians, such as House members Barbara Lee and Dennis Kucinich, take a principled stand against intervention. Writing in *The Nation* magazine, Representative Kucinich, Democrat from Cleveland, called for negotiations with Iran. "The Administration is escalating tensions with Iran, laying the groundwork for an attack and attempting to make a case to bypass Congressional authorization."[27]

But Kucinich, Lee, and other progressives don't represent the majority within the Democratic Party. In March 2007, House Democrats initially inserted a provision requiring

Congressional approval of any U.S. attack on Iran into the
Iraq war spending bill. But under pressure from conservatives
and the American Israel Public Affairs Committee, the clause
was removed before the House could vote on the bill.[28]

On the other hand, in March 2007, Senator James Webb,
Jr., a conservative Republican from Virginia, introduced separate legislation requiring Congressional approval before the
United States could spend money for military attacks against
Iran. "We need the Congress to be involved in any decision to
commence military activities absent an attack from the other
side or a direct threat," said Senator Webb.[29]

Webb and a few other Republican congressmen hold anti-
interventionist views. They had also opposed Bill Clinton's
1999 military attacks against ex-Yugoslavia. The Republican
Party has a small isolationist wing that opposes some U.S.
military interventions. Conservative columnist and one-time
presidential candidate Pat Buchanan strongly condemned
mainstream conservatives for supporting an attack on Iran.[30]
Buchanan and other isolationists impact the views of some
mainstream Republican officials.

So the traditional liberal-versus-conservative, Democrat-
versus-Republican framework doesn't apply to Iran. Conservative corporate interests, right-wing think tanks, and the
pro-Israel lobby pressure both parties to take a hard line
against Iran. Peace groups, a sector of Iranian-Americans, and
progressive think tanks urge alternative strategies.

Is There Another Way?

Mainstream policy makers argue that the United States can't
live with a clerical government in Tehran. They think the

Iranian government will never give up its nuclear ambitions, seek peace with the United States, stop supporting terrorism, or agree to a Palestinian-Israeli settlement. Well, in fact, Iranian authorities once offered to do just that.

In the spring of 2003, Iran contacted Swiss Ambassador Tim Guldimann, who represented the USA diplomatically in Tehran, and proposed comprehensive negotiations that could resolve many of the outstanding U.S.-Iranian issues. The United States had just invaded Iraq, and Iran was worried. In a proposal approved by Supreme Leader Khamenei, Iran agreed to provide intelligence information from Al Qaeda suspects being detained in Iran, agreed to stringent international inspections of nuclear sites, offered to stop military support for Hizbollah and Hamas, and agreed to support a two-state solution to the Israeli-Palestine issue.[31]

The written proposal from Ambassador Guldimann was both faxed and hand delivered to the U.S. State Department. It was promptly ignored by the Bush Administration. The neoconservative faction argued that the United States shouldn't have any dealings with supporters of terrorism. Condoleezza Rice and other Bush officials later denied ever receiving the offer, but receipt of the proposal was confirmed by Flynt Leverett, an analyst with the National Security Council, and by Lawrence Wilkerson, Colin Powell's chief of staff.[32]

We can't know if the Iranians would have negotiated in good faith in 2003. But the Bush Administration didn't even try. It has a history of similar blunders. Starting from its opening months in power, at a time when North Korea did not have nuclear weapons, the Bush Administration unilaterally undercut a 1994 U.S.-Korean agreement that had been negotiated under Bill Clinton. In February 2007, Bush officials went back and negotiated essentially the same agreement—except by then, North Korea had the Bomb.[33]

Successive Democratic and Republican administrations have made a mess of U.S.-Iranian relations since 1979. The United States has tried economic embargoes, UN resolutions, propaganda broadcasts, covert terrorist attacks, detainment of Iranian diplomats living in Iraq, and strident military threats. None have resulted in significant changes inside Iran.

A number of leading experts suggest an alternative. The people of Iran must be left alone to change the government as they see fit. Meanwhile, the United States must negotiate with Iran as part of lowering tensions throughout the Middle East.

Former national security advisor Zbigniew Brzezinski told the Senate Foreign Relations Committee that the United States must leave Iraq "in a reasonably short period of time," start an energetic effort to reach an Israeli-Palestinian peace, and hold a conference on regional stability that includes Iran. In an unusually frank statement for a former National Security Administration chief, Brzezinski said, "Practically no country in the world shares the Manichean delusions that the Administration so passionately articulates. The result is growing political isolation of and pervasive popular antagonism toward the U.S. global posture."[34]

Former CIA official Pillar told me, "I believe it is a big mistake not to engage the Iranians. . . . Among the parallel interests are overall stability in their neck of the woods. We worked together in Afghanistan after the overthrow of the Taliban. The Iranians wanted to have something like that happen in Iraq."[35]

Sane voices in Washington can help lower tensions with

Iran. But I personally don't trust mainstream politicians, lob-byists, and think tank gurus to resolve anything soon. Nor do I trust the clerics in Tehran to stop their belligerence. A pro-peace, pro-democracy movement exists within Iran. I think people in the United States need to build one as well.

The antiwar Iraq movement has already begun educating people about Iran. We need more educational events, people-to-people exchanges, demonstrations, and anti-intervention votes by city governments, all of which can build grassroots pressure to change U.S. policy.[36]

If the governments of the United States and Iran won't make peace, the people of our two countries must.

Acknowledgments

Many people contributed directly and indirectly to the writing of this book.

Omid Memarian is an incredibly talented Iranian journalist who was chief researcher. He is studying at the Graduate School of Journalism at the University of California, Berkeley. Having grown up in Iran as part of that country's younger generation, he provided important insights about current conditions in Iran, as well as contemporary history.

PoliPointPress editor Peter Richardson offered invaluable help in shaping the story. He does what a good editor should do: read the material with a fresh eye and offer constructive suggestions. I first met University of Southern California Professor Muhammad Sahimi when I interviewed him for the book. We subsequently coauthored an article together, and he offered excellent suggestions about the manuscript. My sister Janyce Erlich Moss, a professional photographer and university lecturer in the Washington DC area, shot the author's photo.

My thanks to all the people kind enough to read the manuscript and offer comments, including Omid Memarian, Muhammad Sahimi, Parvis Shokat, Sepideh Koosha, Ahmad Taghvai, Jaleh Behroozi, Hossein Khosrowjah, Dariush Zahedi, and Norman Solomon.

Reese Erlich
Oakland, California
May 2007

Notes

1. In Tehran with Sean Penn

1. My experience is that Iranians approached randomly on the street are about as willing to talk as Americans. I asked interviewees if they wanted to use their full names. Often if sensitive political questions were asked, they preferred to use first names only. Our interview with Moshtabor took place June 11, 2005, in Tehran.

2. While those of us born before 1965 vividly remember the reign of Shah Mohammad Reza Pahlavi, I realize than many younger readers do not. The shah (king) was crowned with British backing in 1941. A democratic movement in parliament restricted his powers in the early 1950s, but he was restored to full power in a CIA-led coup in 1953. The shah ran a brutal dictatorship until 1979, when he was overthrown by a popular revolution.

3. I describe the 1988 USS *Vincennes* incident in greater detail in Chapter 4.

4. I go into much greater detail about the antagonism between Iran and Al Qaeda and the Taliban in Chapter 4.

5. Charles W. Freeman, Jr., interview with author, Jan. 19, 2007, Washington DC.

6. Estimates vary about which countries are number one or two in

oil and gas reserves, depending on how the figures are computed. Iran clearly has some of the largest oil and natural gas reserves in the world. Iran has oil reserves of 133 billion barrels and natural gas reserves of 26.6 trillion cubic meters, according to the CIA's *World Factbook—Iran*, which is available online.

7. Paul Pillar, interview with author, Jan. 18, 2007, Washington DC.

8. Robert Hunter, comments posted on Gulf 2000 list serve, Mar. 2, 2007, quoted with permission.

9. Norman Solomon provides numerous examples of the lies used to justify previous U.S. wars. Norman Solomon, *War Made Easy*, chapter 3 (New York: John Wiley and Sons, 2005).

10. Mohammed Hashemi, interview with author, June 11, 2005, Tehran.

11. Hassan Khomeini, interview with author, June 11, 2005, Tehran.

12. Hamid-Reza Asefi, interview with author, June 12, 2005, Tehran.

13. Interview with author, June 14, 2005, Tehran. This dialogue appeared in my radio documentary "On the Ground in Iran," *Making Contact Radio*, Aug. 24, 2005 (http://www.radioproject.org/archive/2005/3405.html).

14. Sean Penn's series in the *San Francisco Chronicle* began Aug. 22, 2005, and can be viewed online at www.sfgate.com.

15. Charles W. Freeman, Jr., interview with author, Jan. 19, 2007, Washington DC.

2. United States Tells Iran: Become a Nuclear Power

1. James Woolsey, quoted in Thomas Stauffer, "Unlike Dimona, Iran's Bushehr Reactor Not Useful for Weapons-Grade Plutonium," *Washington Report on Middle East Affairs*, Sept. 2003, pp. 28–29.

2. Henry Kissinger, *Washington Post*, Mar. 29, 2005, op-ed article.

3. Dafna Linzer, "Past Arguments Don't Square With Current Iran Policy," *Washington Post*, Mar. 27, 2005.

4. Muhammad Sahimi, interview with author, Oct. 17, 2006, Los Angeles.

5. John K. Cooley, "More Fingers on Nuclear Trigger?" *Christian Science Monitor*, June 25, 1974. See also Elaine Sciolino, "Nuclear Ambitions Aren't New for Iran," *New York Times*, June 22, 2003.

6. *Der Spiegel*, Feb. 8, 1975, as cited in Muhammad Sahimi, "Iran's Nuclear Program, Part V," *Pavand Iran News*, Dec. 22, 2004 (www.pavand.com).

7. Linzer, *Washington Post*.

8. David Wallechinsky and Irving Wallace, *The People's Almanac*, 1981 (http://www.trivia-library.com/c/excesses-of-the-rich-and-wealthy-shah-of-iran-party.htm).

9. Federal Research Service, "The Dhofar Rebellion," *Persian Gulf States: Oman* (Library of Congress, 1993).

10. "Background information on the crisis in Iran," Institute for Policy Studies, Washington DC, 1979 (http://www.irvl.net/USMI .htm).

11. "Electricity in Iran" http://www.sedona.net/pahlavi/electric .html.

12. Hermidas Bavand, interview with author, June 15, 2005, Tehran.

13. Nuclear Threat Initiative (NTI), "Nuclear Chronology 1957–1985," *Iran Country Profile* (www.nti.org/e_research/profiles/1825 _1826.html).

14. Richard Helms, "Issues and Talking Points: Intensified Bilateral Cooperation," *Department of State Brief*, Digital National Security Archive (http://nsarchive.chadwyck.com/marketing/index.jsp).

15. Alexander Montgomery, *Social Action: Rogue Reaction*, Ph.D. thesis, Stanford University, Sept. 2005, p. 163.

16. Nuclear Threat Initiative (NTI), "Nuclear Overview," *Iran Country Profile*, May 1, 2006 (www.nti.org/e_research/profiles/ Iran/index_1822.html). See also Sciolino, *New York Times*, June 22, 2003.

17. Nuclear Threat Initiative.

18. Sahimi interview.

19. Linzer, *Washington Post*. Also, Alfred L. Atherton, "Strategy for your visit to Iran," confidential Department of State Briefing Memorandum, Oct. 20, 1974, in Digital National Security Archive (http://nsarchive.chadwyck.com/marketing/index.jsp).

20. Mohamed ElBaradei, interview for radio documentary *Lessons from Hiroshima 60 Years Later*, Reese Erlich producer, May 2, 2005 (excerpts from the interview available online at www.peacetalks online.org/NoMoreHiroshima/HiroshimaSummary.htm).

21. Montgomery, Ph.D. thesis, p. 159.

22. Muhammad Sahimi, "Iran's Nuclear Energy Program: Part IV," Dec. 7, 2004, www.pavand.com. Sahimi points out that Iran's oil production had declined from 5.8 million barrels per day in 1974 to 3.9 million in 2004, and that the oil fields are far more depleted today than during the shah's time.

23. Associated Press, "Iran Oil Revenue Quickly Drying Up, Analysis Says," *Washington Post*, Dec. 26, 2006.

24. William Broad and Elaine Sciolino, "Iran's Secrecy Widens Gap in Nuclear Intelligence," *New York Times*, May 19, 2006.

25. Sahimi interview.

26. Robert Collier, "Nuclear Weapons Unholy, Iran Says Islam Forbids Use, Clerics Proclaim," *San Francisco Chronicle*, Oct. 31, 2003.

27. Steve Coll, "The Atomic Emporium," *The New Yorker*, Aug. 7 & 14, 2006.

28. IAEA Director General's Report, *Implementation of the NPT Safeguards Agreement in the Islamic Republic of Iran*, Aug. 31, 2006.

29. William Broad and David E. Sanger, "Restraints Fray and Risks Grow As Nuclear Club Gains Members, *New York Times*, Oct. 15, 2006.

30. Mark D. Skootsky, "US Nuclear Policy Toward Iran," June 1, 1995, p. 3, http://people.csail.mit.edu/boris/iran-nuke.text.

31. Dafna Linzer, "Iran Is Judged 10 Years from Nuclear Bomb," *Washington Post*, Aug. 2, 2005.

32. Greg Myre, "Abbas Repeats Call for Vote as Truce Erodes," *New York Times*, Dec. 19, 2006.

33. I explain the military issues between Iran and Israel in Chapter 3.

34. George W. Bush, Rose Garden Press Conference, Apr. 28, 2006, http://www.whitehouse.gov/news/releases/2006/04/print/20060428-2 .html.

35. IAEA Director General's Report.

36. IAEA Director General's Report.

37. Elaine Sciolino, "Highly Enriched Uranium Is Found at an Iranian Plant," *New York Times*, Sept. 1, 2006.

38. Thom Shanker, "Security Council Votes to Tighten Iran Sanctions," *New York Times*, Mar. 25, 2007.

39. Associated Press wire report, Mar. 9, 2006, printed in *Pocatello Idaho State Journal*, Mar. 14, 2006.

40. U.S. State Department, "State Sponsors of Terror Overview," *Country Reports on Terrorism*, chapter 6, Apr. 28, 2006.

41. William Broad and David E. Sanger, "Restraints Fray and Risks Grow as Nuclear Club Gains Members," *New York Times*, Oct. 15, 2006.

42. Some mainstream analysts advocate a similar negotiating position. Ray Takeyh, senior fellow at the Council on Foreign Relations, wrote "Time for Détente with Iran," *Foreign Affairs*, Mar.-Apr. 2007, p. 29.

43. Nuclear Age Peace Foundation, www.nuclearfiles.org.

44. Muhammad Sahimi, "Iran's Nuclear Energy Program: Part IV." Sahimi estimates total nonnuclear alternative energy sources could meet 25 percent of Iran's needs under current conditions.

45. Norman Solomon, Sean Penn, and I interviewed dozens of Iranians we met on the street in June 2005. Not a single one opposed the development of nuclear power. The antinuclear-power position is equated with support for the United States. Absent U.S. threats, a real discussion could take place on the pros and cons of nuclear power.

46. Akbar Ganji, interview with author, July 30, 2006, Berkeley CA.

47. Muhammad Sahimi, "Iran's Nuclear Energy Program: Part VI."

3. Iran, Hizbollah, and Israel: The Real Story

1. In what became known as the Iran-Contra scandal, the administration of President Ronald Reagan sent missiles and other armaments to Iran in return for Iran's using its influence to release U.S.

hostages held in war-torn Lebanon. Administration officials then used the profits from these sales to illegally fund the right-wing Contra guerrillas, who carried out terrorist bombings and assassinations against the elected leftist government of Nicaragua.

2. Eliahu Ben-Elissar, interview with author, June 23, 1987, Jerusalem.

3. Ben-Elissar. See also Reese Erlich, "Behind Israel's Role in the Iran-Contra Arms Scandal," *San Francisco Chronicle*, Aug. 26, 1987.

4. National Security Archive, *The Chronology, the Documented Day-by-Day Account of the Secret Military Assistance to Iran and the Contras*, p. 116 (Warner Books, 1987).

5. Cited in Trita Parsi, "Teheran and Jerusalem Are Not Natural Enemies," South Asia Analysis Group (www.saag.org/Bb/view.asp ?msgID=27964).

6. "Peres: Treat Ahmadinejad like Hitler," *Israel Today*, Oct. 22, 2006 (http://www.israeltoday.co.il/default.aspx?tabid=178&nid =9919).

7. Jewish Task Force, "Fighting to save America and Israel from Islamic terrorism," www.jtf.org/israel/israel.arab.moderates.part.one .htm. The Web page accuses Egypt's presidents Gamal Abdel Nasser and Anwar Sadat and other Arab leaders of being pro-Nazi.

8. On April 2, 2006, on CNN's *Late Edition with Wolf Blitzer*, Iran's Ambassador to the International Atomic Energy Agency Ali Asghar Soltanieh was asked about Iran's position on Israel and Jews.

Blitzer: But should there be a state of Israel?

Soltanieh: I think I've already answered to you. If Israel is a synonym and will give the indication of Zionism mentality, no. But if you are going to conclude that we have said the people there have to be removed or we they have to be massacred or so, this is fabricated, unfortunate selective approach to what the mentality and policy of Islamic Republic of Iran is. I have to correct, and I did so. (http://transcripts.cnn.com/ TRANSCRIPTS/0604/02/le.01.html)

9. Former president Mohammad Khatami advocates a two-state solution. Supreme Leader Khamenei offered to support a two-state

solution in a 2003 proposal sent to the Bush Administration through the Swiss ambassador to Iran. For details, see Chapter 11.

10. Scott MacLeod, "We Do Not Need Attacks," *Time*, Sept. 17, 2006.

11. www.al-bab.com/arab/docs/league/peace02.htm.

12. Ahmed Yousef, senior advisor to the Hamas prime minister of the Palestinian Authority, "Pause for Peace," op-ed commentary, *New York Times*, Nov. 1, 2006.

13. Cam Simpson, "Israeli Citizens Struggle Amid Iran's Nuclear Vow," *Wall Street Journal*, Dec. 26, 2006.

14. Mohammed Raad, interview with author, June 27, 2003, southern Lebanon.

15. Farid El Khazen, interview with author, July 30, 1998, Beirut.

16. Ali Nouri Zadeh, "Iranians Upset at Government's Financial Aid to Hizbollah in Lebanon," *Asharq Alawsat* (Arabic newspaper in London), Aug. 21, 2006 (http://aawsat.com/english/news.asp?section=1&id=6077).

17. Maziar Bahari, "Sweating Out the Truth in Iran," *International Herald Tribune*, op-ed page, Aug. 25, 2006.

18. Israel withdrew unilaterally from Gaza in September 2005 but continued to economically strangle the territory by prohibiting sea, air, and land access. Palestinians were rarely allowed outside Gaza to work in Israel. On June 25, 2006, Palestinian militants attacked an Israeli post just outside Gaza and captured a soldier. That led directly to Israel's re-occupation of parts of Gaza a few days later.

19. Human Rights Watch, "Israel: More Evidence on Beach Killings Implicates IDF," *Human Rights News*, June 15, 2006 (http://hrw.org/english/docs/2006/06/15/isrlpa13570.htm).

20. Seymour Hersh, "Watching Lebanon, Washington's interests in Israel's war," *The New Yorker*, Aug. 21, 2006.

21. Hersh, Aug. 21, 2006.

22. Meron Rappaport, "IDF Commander: We Fired More Than a Million Cluster Bombs in Lebanon," *Haaretz* (Israeli daily newspaper), Sept. 12, 2006. See also "Official: Israel Used Phosphorous Bombs," AP wire story, *USA Today*, Oct. 23, 2006.

23. Human Rights Watch, "Lebanon/Israel: Hizbollah Hit Israel

with Cluster Munitions During Conflict," *Human Rights News*, Oct. 19, 2006 (http://hrw.org/english/docs/2006/10/18/lebano14412.htm).

24. David S. Cloud and Greg Myre, "Israel May Have Violated Arms Pact, U.S. Officials Say," *New York Times*, Jan. 28, 2007.

25. Rory McCarthy, "Cluster Bombing of Lebanon 'Immoral' UN Official Tells Israel," *The Guardian* (London), Aug. 31, 2006.

26. Human Rights Watch, Oct. 19, 2006.

27. Human Rights Watch, Oct. 19, 2006.

28. Steven Erlanger, "Israeli Admits Big Errors in Lebanon War, but Won't Resign," *New York Times*, Jan. 3, 2007.

29. "Mideast War, by the Numbers," AP wire story, Aug. 18, 2006.

30. Neil King, Jr., "War Emboldens Iran Ahead of Nuclear Talks," *Wall Street Journal*, Aug. 16, 2006.

4. A Brief History of U.S.-Iranian Relations

1. Quoted in Stephen Kinzer, *All the Shah's Men*, p. 40 (New York: John Wiley & Sons, 2003).

2. Radio documentary *The Struggle for Iran*, produced by Reese Erlich for KQED Radio News and distributed nationally on NPR stations, 2001 (http://www.iranproject.org). The media segment quoted here was reported by Deepa Fernandes.

3. Kinzer, *All the Shah's Men*, p. 67.

4. Kinzer, *All the Shah's Men*, p. 155.

5. Kinzer, *All the Shah's Men*, p. 160.

6. CIA, *Clandestine Service History, Overthrow of Premier Mossadeq of Iran*, p. 37, available online from the *New York Times* (www.nytimes.com/library/world/mideast/041600iran-cia-index.html).

7. CIA, *Clandestine Service History*, p. 59.

8. Kinzer, *All the Shah's Men*, p. 178.

9. Kinzer, *All the Shah's Men*, p. 190.

10. Radio documentary *The Struggle for Iran*.

11. Mark Gasiorowski, "Just Like That: How the Mossadegh Government Was Overthrown," *The Iranian*, Apr. 19, 2000 (www.gwu.edu/~nsarchiv/NSAEBB/NSAEBB28/index.html).

12. "Statements on Iranian Oil Accord," AP wire story, Aug. 6, 1954.

13. Institute for Policy Studies, "Background Information on the Crisis in Iran," Washington DC, 1979.

14. Hoover Institution, *Great Expectations: Democracy in Iran*, Apr. 28, 2003 (www.hoover.org/publications/uk/3001451.html).

15. Human rights activist and historian Emad Baghi estimated 88 were killed on Black Friday. Cited in Cyrus Kadivar, "A Question of Numbers," Rouzegar-Now, Aug. 8, 2003 (www.emadbaghi.com/en/archives/000592.php).

16. Massoumeh Ebtekar, interview with author, Nov. 1, 2000, Tehran. Ebtekar wrote a book about her experiences, entitled *Takeover in Tehran* (Vancouver: Talon Books, 2000).

17. Barry Rosen, interview with author, Sept. 6, 2000, New York. Rosen's description also appears in the radio documentary *The Struggle for Iran.*

18. Ebtekar interview.

19. Abbas Abdi, interview with author, Nov. 1, 2000, Tehran.

20. Robert Parry, "The Original October Surprise," Consortium news.com, Oct. 25, 2006 (www.consortiumnews.com/2006/102506 .html). Parry quotes from former Iranian president Banisadr, who goes into great detail about Iran's negotiations with Republican leaders prior to the November 1980 election.

21. The Algiers Agreement legally prohibits the United States from attacking Iran, something conveniently forgotten by both leading Democrats and Republicans during later Iran crises.

22. Bob Woodward, *Veil*, p. 412 (New York: Simon and Shuster, 1987).

23. "July 3, 1988, Defense Department Briefing on Current Developments in the Persian Gulf." Early U.S. media reports simply echoed the claims by the Defense Department that an "Iranian aircraft" had attacked the *Vincennes*, not mentioning that it was a civilian airliner. By 1:30 p.m. EDT, William J. Crowe, Jr., Chairman, Joint Chiefs of Staff, admitted in a press conference that it was a civilian plane but asserted that the *Vincennes* fired in self-defense.

24. Ronald Reagan, Statement on the Destruction of an Iranian Jetliner by the United States Navy Over the Persian Gulf, July 3, 1988.

25. Ted Koppel, *Nightline*, July 1, 1992. *Newsweek* and ABC's *Nightline* did a joint investigative report exposing the Navy's misinformation.

26. John Barry and Roger Charles, "Sea of Lies," *Newsweek*, July 13, 1992.

27. In Nicaragua in the 1980s, the USA trained and financially supported Contra groups, which systematically murdered teachers, medical personnel, and other civilians in an effort to destroy Sandinista reforms in the countryside. The United States has used similar tactics in Chile, Iran, Lebanon, South Vietnam, and numerous other countries.

28. GlobalSecurity.Org, "Khobar Towers Bombing" (www.global security.org/security/profiles/khobar_towers_bombing.htm).

29. Iranian intelligence agents murdered Kurdish opposition leaders in Vienna in 1989 and Berlin in 1992, and former prime minister Shapour Bakhtiar in Paris in 1991.

30. Gary Sick, "Iran: Confronting Terrorism," *Washington Quarterly*, Autumn 2003.

31. Wilfried Buchta, *Who Rules Iran?* p. 147 (Washington DC: Washington Institute for Near East Policy and the Konrad Adenauer Stiftung, 2000).

32. Agence France Press, Dec. 6, 2001, cited in *Washington Quarterly*.

33. Sick, *Washington Quarterly*.

5. Who Rules Iran?

1. Sean Penn, "Sean Penn in Iran," Day 2, *San Francisco Chronicle*, Aug. 23, 2005. The entire five-part series is available online at www.sfgate.com/cgi-bin/article.cgi?f=/c/a/2005/08/22/DDGJUEAF 041.DTL. It's a good, very personal introduction to Iranian politics and the Iranian opposition.

2. Gareth Smyth, "Larijani's Pragmatist Reputation Faces Severe Challenge," *Financial Times*, Jan. 10, 2006.

3. Gareth Smyth, "Fundamentalists, Pragmatists, and the Rights of the Nation: Iranian Politics and Nuclear Confrontation," *Century Foundation Report* (www.tcf.org/list.asp?type=PB&pubid=597).

4. Transparency International, 2006 Corruption Perceptions Index, www.infoplease.com/ipa/A0781359.html.

5. Darius Bazargan, "Iran: Politics, the Military and Gulf Security," *Middle East Review of International Affairs Journal*, Sept. 1997.

6. Statement of Kenneth Katzman, specialist in Middle Eastern Affairs, Congressional Reserach Service, before Joint Economic Hearing on Iran, July 26, 2006.

7. Paul Klebnikov, "Millionaire Mullahs," *Forbes Magazine*, July 7, 2003.

8. Robert D. Kaplan, "A Bazaari's World," *The Atlantic Monthly*, Mar. 1996.

9. In February 1989 Ayatollah Khomeini issued a fatwa (religious directive) accusing British novelist Salman Rushdie of blasphemy for insulting the prophet Mohammad, and Khomeini called for his assassination. Supreme Leader Ayatollah Khamenei reaffirmed the fatwa in 2005 although, apparently, there have been no efforts to carry it out in recent years.

10. Mohsen Sazegara, "What Was Once a Revolutionary Guard Is Now Just a Mafia," *Jewish Daily Forward*, Mar. 16, 2007.

11. Smyth, "Larijani's Pragmatist Reputation Faces Severe Challenge."

12. Ted Koppel, "An Offer Tehran Can't Refuse," *New York Times*, op-ed, Oct. 2, 2006.

13. Hooshang Amirahmadi, interview with author, Oct. 7, 2006, Berkeley CA.

14. Vali Nasr and Ali Gheissari, "Foxes in Iran's Henhouse," *New York Times*, op-ed, Dec. 13, 2004.

15. For a full transcript of Albright's speech, see www.gasandoil.com/goc/speeches/albright-17-03-00.htm.

16. The fact that the Clinton Administration wanted to begin a dialogue was no guarantee that the USA would have ultimately agreed to normalize relations with Iran. Powerful conservative forces within the U.S. ruling elite, particularly the pro-Israel lobby, oppose any rapprochement with Iran. Under Clinton, the USA imposed additional unilateral economic sanctions on Iran.

17. Human Rights Watch, "Pour-Mohammadi and the 1998 Seri-

al Murders of Dissident Intellectuals," http://hrw.org/backgrounder/mena/iran1205/3.htm.

18. Sources vary on the number of students killed. Ali Akbar Mahdi says five were murdered in "The Student Movement in the Islamic Republic of Iran," *Journal of Iranian Research and Analysis*, Nov. 1999.

19. CNN, "Rafsanjani to Face Tehran Mayor," CNN.com, June 18, 2005.

20. Amirahmadi, interview with author.

21. Nazila Fathi, "Iran Lifts Ban Barring Women from Attending Sporting Events, *New York Times*, May 1, 2006.

22. Abbas Milani, "Iran's New President," *Hoover Digest*, No. 4, 2005. See also Robert Lowe and Claire Spencer, editors, *Iran, Its Neighbours and the Regional Crises*, p. 13 (London: Royal Institute of International Affairs, 2006).

23. Amirahmadi, interview with author.

24. The Expediency Council mediates disputes between parliament and the Guardian Council. Rafsanjani uses his position as head of the Expediency Council to keep himself in the public eye.

6. Who Will Be Iran's Next Ruler?

1. Reza Pahlavi, interview with author, Jan. 16, 2007, McLean VA.

2. Reza Pahlavi, interview with author.

3. Paul Pillar, interview with author, Jan. 18, 2007, Washington DC.

4. The USA claims Americans are threatened by everyone from real terrorist groups (Al Qaeda) to groups that have used terrorist tactics but are considered legitimate political parties in their homeland (Hizbollah in Lebanon), to Marxist guerrillas (Revolutionary Armed Forces of Colombia) who stand opposed to Muslim fundamentalists. If all those groups get together in one room, I sure hope none of them are armed.

5. Connie Bruck, "Exiles," *The New Yorker*, Mar. 6, 2006.

6. Mohsen Sazegara, interview with Council on Foreign Relations, Oct. 20, 2006, www.sazegara.net/english/archives/2006/10/sazegara_strong.html.

7. Laura Rozen, "Has Washington Found Its Iranian Chalabi?" *Mother Jones* Web site, Oct. 6, 2006 (http://www.motherjones.com/news/feature/2006/11/fakhravar.html).

8. The U.S. justification for listing the MEK as a foreign terrorist organization can be found at http://www.state.gov/s/ct/rls/crt/2005/65275.htm.

9. Reese Erlich, "The Celibates of Ocalan," *Mother Jones*, Mar.-Apr. 2007.

10. "Mojahedin Members' Families Meet in Baghdad to Free Their Children," Iran-Interlink News, July 17, 2003 (www.iran-interlink.org/files/child%20pages/families%2017july.htm).

11. Massoud Khodabandeh, phone interview with author, Jan. 22, 2007, London.

12. Abraham Sofaer, phone interview with author, Nov. 11, 2006, Stanford University, CA.

13. Shahram Homayoun, interview with author, Oct. 17, 2006, Los Angeles.

14. Bijan Khalili, interview with author, Oct. 16, 2006, Los Angeles.

15. Ali Mostashari and Ali Khodamhosseini, "An Overview of Socioeconomic Characteristics of the Iranian-American Community Based on the 2000 U.S. Census," Feb. 2004, Iranian Studies Group, MIT (http://isg-mit.org/projects-storage/census/socioeconomic.pdf).

16. Khalili, interview with author.

17. Amir Shadjareh, interview with author, Oct. 16, 2006.

18. Homayoun, interview with author.

19. Hakha press release, May 27, 2005, www.ahura.info/pressroom/pressrelease_06022005.html.

20. See for example the Web site Regime Change Iran (http://regimechangeiniran.com/2005/06/hakha-movement-overthrow-of-th/).

21. Larry Cohler-Esses, "Yellow Journalism: Anatomy of a Hoax," *The Jewish Week* (New York), May 25, 2006 (http://thejewishweek.com/news/newscontent.php3?artid=12511).

22. "Our Mistake: Note to Readers," *National Post*, May 24, 2006 (www.canada.com/nationalpost/news/story.html?id=6df3e493-f350-4b53-bc16-53262b49a4f7).

23. Homayoun, interview with author.

24. Cohler-Esses, *The Jewish Week.*

25. Abbas Milani, interview with author, Oct. 5, 2006, Palo Alto CA.

26. U.S. State Department fact sheet, issued Feb. 15, 2006, Washington DC (www.state.gov/r/pa/prs/ps/2006/61268.htm).

7. Iran's Democratic Opposition

1. Omid Memarian, "Nobel Peace Winner Threatened with Arrest," Inter Press Service, Aug. 28, 2006.

2. Shirin Ebadi, interview with author, Nov. 15, 2006, Tehran.

3. Karl Vick and David Finkel, "U.S. Push for Democracy Could Backfire Inside Iran," *Washington Post*, Mar. 14, 2006.

4. Akbar Ganji, interview with author, Aug. 3, 2006, Ross CA.

5. Akbar Ganji, interview with author, July 30, 2006, Berkeley CA.

6. Ebadi, interview with author.

7. Ali Mohammadi, interview with author, Nov. 13, 2006, Tehran.

8. Human Rights Watch, "Pour-Mohammadi and the 1988 Prison Massacres," Dec. 2005, http://www.hrw.org/backgrounder/mena/iran1205/2.htm.

9. *The Struggle for Iran*, produced by Reese Erlich, can be heard online at www.iranproject.org/.

10. Ali Afshari, interview with author, Oct. 26, 2000.

11. Afshari now does analysis for Voice of America. Amnesty International detailed his forced confession, "Iran: Student leader forced to 'confess' on television," available at http://www.web.amnesty.org/web/wwa.nsf/print/irn-011002-wwa-eng.

12. Nazila Fathi, "Iran President Facing Revival of Students' Ire," *New York Times*, Dec. 21, 2006.

13. Forugh Farrokhzad's Open Forum Web Site (www.forughfarrokhzad.com/selectedworks/main.asp).

14. Pouran Farrokhzad, interview with author, Nov. 15, 2006, Tehran.

15. "Execution of a Teenage Girl," BBC Web site, July 27, 2006.

16. Shirin Ebadi's group, the Center for the Defense of Human Rights, and Amnesty International, among others, have taken up the campaign to stop stoning (http://amnesty.org.uk/news_details.asp ?NewsID=17211).

17. The One Million Signatures Demanding Changes to Discriminatory Laws Web site is www.we-change.org. It publishes in several languages.

18. Amnesty International, "Facts and Figures on the Death Penalty," http://web.amnesty.org/pages/deathpenalty-facts-eng.

19. Emad Baghi, interview with author, Nov. 18, 2006, Tehran.

20. Nazila Fathi, "Iran Says Sunnis, Using Pakistan as Base, Planned Fatal Bombing," *New York Times*, Feb. 29, 2007.

21. Brian Ross and Christopher Isham, "The Secret War Against Iran," *ABC Evening News*, Apr. 3, 2007.

22. Seymour Hersh, "The Next Act," *The New Yorker*, Nov. 11, 2006.

23. For a listing of all U.S. sanctions against Iran, see Kenneth Katzman, "Iran: U.S. Concerns and Policy Responses," *Congressional Research Service Report for Congress*, Jan. 5, 2007.

24. Ebrahim Yazdi, interview with author, Nov. 16, 2006, Tehran.

8. Iran's Ethnic Minorities: Rebellion on the Borders

1. As'ad Ardalan, interview with author, Nov. 16, 2006, Tehran.

2. Hamidreza Jalaeipour, a leading reformist and former government official in Kurdistan in the 1980s, wrote an analysis of the unsuccessful Kurdish rebellion against the central government that lasted from 1979 to 1988. He criticizes the Kurdish movement, and by extension all ethnic minorities. He wrote that had the Kurds rejected autonomy and kept their struggle confined to the "provisions of the Islamic Republic of Iran's constitution, their struggle would have been more peaceful, less costly for Kurds and Kurdistan would have better developed." Hamidreza Jalaeipour, academic paper, *The Rise and Decline of Kurdish Movement in Years 1978–88*.

3. Edward N. Luttwak, "Persian Shrug," *Wall Street Journal*, op-ed page, Feb. 27, 2007.

4. Iranian ethnic leaders say minorities actually total over half the population, arguing the state census figures undercount their numbers. Such claims can't be verified without a freely conducted census, however, so I've used the CIA research figures. CIA, *The World Fact Book*, 2006, https://www.cia.gov/.

5. The estimate of 300,000 Bahais comes from the Bahai International Community based in the USA (http://info.bahai.org/persecution _iran.html).

6. Abbas Milani, interview with author, Oct. 5, 2006, Palo Alto CA.

7. Estimates of the total number of Kurds in the four countries run from 27 to 36 million because of inaccurate census counts. Ralph Peters, "Blood Borders," *Armed Forces Journal*, June 2006.

8. Walter Posch, "Islamist Neo-Cons Take Power in Iran," Ljubljana Institute for Security Studies, *Occasional Paper No. 3*, July 2005.

9. Frances Harrison, "Iran Press Reports Kurdish Riots," *BBC News* Web site, July 7, 2005.

10. Mustafa Hejri, interview with author, Nov. 24, 2006, Koya, Iraq.

11. Morteza Esfandiari, phone interview with author, Jan. 5, 2007, Washington DC.

12. Information about the KDP-I is based on follow-up interviews done by Yerevan Adham in December 2006. He helped me arrange interviews and translated during my trip to northern Iraq in 2006.

13. Mohtadi, interview with author.

14. Lt. Col. Dennis Chapman, interview with author, Nov. 21, 2006, Suleimanyah, Iraq.

15. Seymour Hersh, "The Next Act," *The New Yorker*, Nov. 27, 2006.

16. The State Department's justification for listing PKK as a foreign terrorist organization can be found at Country Reports on Terrorism, Apr. 28, 2006, http://www.state.gov/s/ct/rls/crt/2005/65275 .htm.

17. Zenar Agri, interview with author, Nov. 26, 2006, PJAK guerrilla base, Qandil mountains, Iraq.

18. Zenar Agri, interview with author.

19. Reese Erlich, "The Celibates of Ocalan," *Mother Jones* magazine, Mar.-Apr. 2007. See also "Tehran Insider Tells of U.S. Black Ops," *Asia Times* Web site, Apr. 26, 2006.

20. Paul Pillar, former CIA national intelligence officer for the Near East and South Asia, interview with author, Jan. 18, 2006, Washington DC.

21. Ardalan, interview with author.

22. Reese Erlich, "Calm amid a Storm," *Dallas Morning News*, Dec. 22, 2006.

23. "Kurdish Soldiers Trained by Israelis," *BBC News* Web site, Sept. 20, 2006.

24. Hersh, *The New Yorker*, Nov. 27, 2006.

25. The Israeli government tried to keep the training secret but reports surfaced inside Israel. See Conal Urquhart and Michael Howard, *The Guardian* (London), Dec. 2, 2005.

26. Esfandiari, interview with author.

27. Reza Salahshour, representative of the World Azerbaijan Congress, told me Turkish-origin Iranians, including Azerbaijanis, make up 52 percent of the Iranian population, a figure not backed up by other credible sources. Phone interview with author, Oct. 23, 2006, Washington DC.

28. On Oct. 12, 2006, the Supreme Leader's personal envoy, Ayatollah Moshen Mujtahed-Shabestari, responded to those who want to secede from Iran, "If there is to be any union, (Azerbaijan) should join Iran." "Iran Adopts Firm Stance on Minority Rights Issue," Eurasianet.org, Oct. 20, 2006.

29. Amnesty International, "Incommunicado Detention, Abbas Lisani," June 8, 2006 (UA 163/06).

30. Nazila Fathi, "Ethnic Tensions Over Cartoon Set Off Riots in Northwest Iran," *New York Times*, May 29, 2006.

31. Salahshour, interview with author.

32. Nayereh Tohidi, "Iran: regionalism, ethnicity and democracy," Open Democracy.net, June 29, 2006.

33. Miloon Kothari, UN Commission on Human Rights Special Rapporteur on Adequate Housing, interview with IRINnews.org, May 2, 2006.

34. Accurate figures were hard to determine because foreign reporters weren't on the scene in Ahwaz. I took my figures from Amnesty International, "Iran: Need for restraint as anniversary of unrest in Khuzestan approaches," Apr. 13, 2006; and also from Islamic Republic News Agency, "Defense Minister praises Arab Iranians' role in sacred defense," May 3, 2005 (www.webneveshteha.com/en/article.asp?id=-1181330580).

35. I explain this case in greater detail in the Chapter 7 section about NGOs.

36. Karim Abdian, executive director of the Ahwaz Human Rights Organization, interview with author, Jan. 15, 2007, Washington DC.

37. Elliot Abrams was heavily involved in the illegal arms and money deals between Iran and Nicaragua. He pled guilty to two counts of withholding information from Congress about the Reagan Administration's illegal aid to the Nicaraguan Contras.

38. Shahin Abbasov, "Iran: Ethnic Azeri Activist Predicts More Protests," Eurasia.net, July 31, 2006.

39. Alireza Nazmi, phone interview with author, Nov. 2, 2006, Tulare CA.

9. What the U.S. Media Didn't Tell You

1. Babak Dehghan Pisheh as quoted by Omid Memarian, "Western Journalists in Iran: Fast Food Stories," Web site presentation for University of California, Berkeley, Graduate School of Journalism, Apr. 26, 2006.

2. Norman Solomon and Reese Erlich, *Target Iraq: What the News Media Didn't Tell You* (New York: Context Books, 2003).

3. Thom Shanker, "U.S. and Britain to Add Ships to Persian Gulf in Signal to Iran," *New York Times*, Dec. 21, 2006.

4. "Iran involvement suspected in Karbala compound attack," CNN.com Web page, Jan. 31, 2007.

5. "Riots erupt in Cyprus over Archbishop," BBC Web site, Mar. 10, 1956 (http://news.bbc.co.uk/onthisday/hi/dates/stories/march/10/newsid_4216000/4216931.stm).

6. Chalmers Johnson, *737 Military Bases = Global Empire* (New York: Metropolitan Books, 2007) excerpted by Alternet.com, Feb. 19,

2007. Johnson noted that the Pentagon simply doesn't count some of its bases, and the real total is closer to 1,000.

7. Ben Bagdikian in his classic book *The New Media Monopoly* (Boston: Beacon Press), describes the process of media consolidation and the dangers it poses to U.S. democracy (www.benbagdikian.com).

8. Public Editor Byron Calame, "Behind the Eavesdropping Story, a Loud Silence," *New York Times*, Week in Review, Jan. 1, 2006; Calame, "Secrecy, Security, the President and the Press," July 2, 2006; Calame, "Eavesdropping and the Election: An Answer on the Question of Timing," *New York Times*, Aug. 13, 2006. The public editor at the *Times* functions like an ombudsperson at other newspapers.

9. CBS *Evening News*, Jan. 29, 2007.

10. Michael R. Gordon, "Deadliest Bomb in Iraq Is Made by Iran, U.S. Says," *New York Times*, Feb. 10, 2007.

11. James Glanz, "U.S. Says Arms Link Iranians to Iraqi Shiites," *New York Times*, Feb. 12, 2007.

12. Patrick Cockburn, "Target Tehran: Washington Sets Stage for a New Confrontation," *Independent* (London), Feb. 12, 2007.

13. Paul Reynolds, "US claims against Iran: Why now?" *BBC News* Web site, Feb. 12, 2007.

14. Alexandra Zavis and Greg Miller, "Scant Evidence Found of Iran-Iraq Arms Link," *Los Angeles Times*, Jan. 23, 2007.

15. The Institute for Public Accuracy (IPA) offered media interviews with two experts who directly criticized the military intelligence. IPA press release, Feb. 13, 2007. See also Reese Erlich and Muhammad Sahimi, "Fabricated Evidence: Round Two?" Truth Dig.org, Mar. 13, 2007.

16. Byron Calame, "Approaching Iran Intelligence with Intelligent Skepticism," *New York Times*, Week in Review, Feb. 25, 2007.

17. The results of this policy are sometimes hilarious. In one article *Times* reporter Nicholas Wood quotes a Western diplomat, "who requested anonymity because he was not permitted to comment on the matter for attribution." In other words, the source remained anonymous because he wanted to remain anonymous. Nicholas Wood, "Serbs to Vote on Document That Is Faulty, Critics Say," *New York Times*, Oct. 23, 2006. In May 2006, the *Times* editors changed the policy, supposedly to allow more flexibility and avoid this kind of

tautology. As noted here, however, this absurd example came out five months after the new policy began.

18. Sara Chayes, quoted in the *Bulletin Online*, Global Security News and Analysis (http://www.thebulletin.org/article.php?art_ofn =so06chayes).

19. *News War*, PBS Frontline TV documentary, aired Feb. 27, 2007.

20. Carlotta Gall, "U.S. Military Investigating Death of Afghan in Custody," *New York Times*, Mar. 4, 2003.

21. Quoted from Eric Umansky's excellent analysis of the failures of major media to expose U.S. use of torture. Eric Umansky, "Failures of Imagination," *Columbia Journalism Review*, Sept.–Oct. 2006.

22. Dana Priest, "CIA Holds Terror Suspects in Secret Prisons," *Washington Post*, Nov. 2, 2005.

23. Do a Google search for "Fidel Castro and Hitler," "Saddam Hussein and Hitler," "Slobodan Milosevic and Hitler," and "Ahmadinejad and Hitler." You'll find an amazing number of media references showing that every few years the United States is threatened by a new Hitler.

24. In early February 2007, astronaut Lisa Nowak allegedly tried to kidnap the girlfriend of her astronaut lover. The cable news networks devoted extensive coverage to the rather bizarre story and made it a major news event right up until former *Playboy* model Anna Nicole Smith died a few days later.

25. Steve Doocy, *Fox and Friends*, Apr. 13, 2006. To view the video clip, see http://www.newshounds.us/2006/04/13/fox_news_spreading _panic_on_iran_nuke_plans.php.

26. Glenn Beck, CNN.com, transcript, Sept. 19, 2006.

27. Glenn Beck, CNN.com, transcript, Nov. 11, 2006.

28. Bill Carter and Jacques Steinberg, "With Anchors Still Settling In, NBC Feels Pressure at the Top," *New York Times*, Mar. 1, 2007.

10. Learning the Lessons of Iraq

1. Norman Solomon and Reese Erlich, *Target Iraq: What the News Media Didn't Tell You*, p. 37 (New York: Context Books, 2003).

2. Norman Solomon and Reese Erlich, *Target Iraq*, pp. 113–5.

3. Zbigniew Brzezinski, testimony before the Senate Foreign Relations Committee, Feb. 1, 2007.

4. Michael Gordon, "Prewar Slide Show Cast Iraq in Rosy Hues," *New York Times*, Feb. 15, 2007. See www.nsarchive.org for the original documents.

5. Charles W. Freeman, Jr., interview with author, Jan. 19, 2007, Washington DC.

6. Michael A. Ledeen, "The Wider War," *Wall Street Journal*, op-ed page, Mar. 3, 2007.

7. My interview with Zuhair Razavi and others in this section first appeared in my article "Iran's Waiting Game," *St. Petersburg Times*, July 3, 2005.

8. Majid Ghammas, interview with author, June 16, 2005.

9. Mehdi Rafsanjani, interview with author, June 11, 2005.

10. Hamid-Reza Asefi, interview with author, June 12, 2005.

11. Philip Zelikow, phone interview with author, Feb. 6, 2007, Charlottesville VA.

12. "Islamic State of Iraq Amir Announces Plans to Counter US Security Plan," Open Source Center—Jihadist Web sites, Feb. 3, 2007.

13. Thomas G. McInerney, "Iran Escalates," *Wall Street Journal*, op-ed page, Mar. 31, 2007.

14. Seymour Hersh, "The Iran Plans," *The New Yorker*, Apr. 17, 2006.

15. Andrew Higgins, "As U.S. Puts Pressure on Iran, Gulf's Religious Rift Spreads," *Wall Street Journal*, Feb. 25, 2007.

16. Seymour Hersh, "The Redirection," *The New Yorker*, Mar. 5, 2007.

17. Peter Hirschberg, "Netanyahu: It's 1938 and Iran Is Germany; Ahmadinejad Is Preparing Another Holocaust," *Haaretz* (Tel Aviv), Dec. 19, 2006.

18. "Focus: Mission Iran," *The Sunday Times* (London), Jan. 7, 2007.

19. Tom Baldwin and Philip Webster, "Fears Grow Over Iran," *The Times* (London), Feb. 23, 2007.

20. James Fallows, "Will Iran Be Next?" *The Atlantic Monthly*, Dec. 2004. Col. Gardiner updated his information in *The End of the*

"Summer of Diplomacy": Assessing U.S. Military Options on Iran (Washington DC: Century Foundation Report, 2006).

21. Paul Pillar, former CIA national intelligence officer for the Near East and South Asia, interview with author, Jan. 18, 2007, Washington DC.

22. President Bashar al-Asad, interview with author, June 11, 2006, Damascus.

23. Abbas Milani, interview with author, Oct. 5, 2006, Palo Alto CA. Milani is the director of Iranian Studies at Stanford University and codirector of the Iran Democracy Project at the Hoover Institution.

24. Associated Press, "Hillary Clinton Calls Iran a Threat to U.S., Israel," AP wire story, Feb. 2, 2007.

25. David E. Sanger, "On Iran, Bush Confronts Haunting Echoes of Iraq," *New York Times*, Jan. 28, 2007.

26. Nancy Pelosi, Speech to the American Israel Public Affairs Committee, May 23, 2005.

27. Dennis Kucinich, "Collision Course with Iran," *The Nation*, Feb. 27, 2007.

28. "AIPAC backed removal of Iran war provision," Jewish Telegraphic Agency, Mar. 13, 2007.

29. Christina Bellantoni, "Webb Bill Limits Iran Fight," *Washington Times*, Mar. 6, 2007.

30. Patrick J. Buchanan, "Of Imperial Presidents and Congressional Cowards," syndicated column, *San Francisco Chronicle*, May 1, 2006.

31. Gareth Porter first broke the story in "Burnt Offering," *The American Prospect*, June 6, 2006. The story was confirmed by Glenn Kessler, "U.S. Missed Chance with Iran, Ex-Officials Claim," *Washington Post*, June 18, 2006.

32. Gareth Porter, "First Rejected, Now Denied," *The American Prospect*, Feb. 9, 2007. See also Kessler, *Washington Post*.

33. Charles Scanlon, "The end of a long confrontation?", *BBC News* Web page, Feb. 13, 2007.

34. Brzezinski testimony.

35. Pillar, interview with author.

36. Some groups working against intervention in Iran and related

issues include Campaign Against Sanctions and Military Intervention in Iran (http://www.campaigniran.org/casmii), Just Foreign Policy (www.justforeignpolicy.org), Global Exchange (www.globalexchange .org), United For Peace and Justice (www.unitedforpeaceandjustice .org), and Jewish Voice for Peace (www.jewishvoiceforpeace.org).

Index

About the Author

Reese Erlich is the coauthor, with Norman Solomon, of the national bestseller *Target Iraq: What the News Media Didn't Tell You* (2003). A freelance print and broadcast reporter, he has covered the Middle East since 1987.

Erlich began his journalism career in 1968 as a staff writer and research editor for *Ramparts*, an investigative reporting magazine based in San Francisco. He taught journalism for ten years at San Francisco State University and California State University, East Bay. His reporting appears in *Mother Jones, Dallas Morning News, San Francisco Chronicle,* and *St. Petersburg Times.* His radio work airs on CBC/Radio-Canada and National Public Radio, among others.

Erlich was a segment producer for the public radio series "Crossing East," a history of Asians in the United States, which received a Peabody Award in 2007. He has also received awards from Project Censored, the Chicago International Film Festival, the Society of Professional Journalists (Northern California), and the Association for Women in Communication. He lives in Oakland, California.

Other Books from PoliPointPress

The Blue Pages: A Directory of Companies Rated by Their Politics and Practices

Helps consumers match their buying decisions with their political values by listing the political contributions and business practices of over 1,000 companies. $9.95, PAPERBACK ORIGINAL.

Jeff Cohen, *Cable News Confidential: My Misadventures in Corporate Media*

Offers a fast-paced romp through the three major cable news channels—Fox, CNN, and MSNBC—and delivers a serious message about their failure to cover the most urgent issues of the day. $14.95, PAPERBACK ORIGINAL.

Marjorie Cohn, *Cowboy Republic: Six Ways the Bush Gang Has Defied the Law*

Shows how the executive branch under President Bush has systematically defied the law instead of enforcing it. $14.95, PAPERBACK ORIGINAL.

Joe Conason, *The Raw Deal: How the Bush Republicans Plan to Destroy Social Security and the Legacy of the New Deal*

Reveals the well-financed and determined effort to undo the Social Security Act and other New Deal programs. $11.00, PAPERBACK ORIGINAL.

Steven Hill, *10 Steps to Repair American Democracy*

Identifies the key problems with American democracy, especially election practices, and proposes ten specific reforms to reinvigorate it. $11.00, PAPERBACK ORIGINAL.

Yvonne Latty, *In Conflict: Iraq War Veterans Speak Out on Duty, Loss, and the Fight to Stay Alive*

Features the unheard voices, extraordinary experiences, and personal photographs of a broad mix of Iraq War veterans, including Congressman Patrick Murphy, Tammy Duckworth, Kelly Daugherty, and Camilo Mejia. $24.00, HARDCOVER.

Phillip Longman, *Best Care Anywhere: Why VA Health Care Is Better Than Yours*

Shows how the turnaround at the long-maligned VA hospitals provides a blueprint for salvaging America's expensive but troubled health care system. $14.95, PAPERBACK ORIGINAL.

William Rivers Pitt, *House of Ill Repute: Reflections on War, Lies, and America's Ravaged Reputation*

Skewers the Bush Administration for its reckless invasions, warrantless wiretaps, lethally incompetent response to Hurricane Katrina, and other scandals and blunders. $16.00, PAPERBACK ORIGINAL.

Nomi Prins, *Jacked: How "Conservatives" Are Picking Your Pocket—Whether You Voted For Them or Not*

Describes how the "conservative" agenda has affected your wallet, skewed national priorities, and diminished America—but not the American spirit. $12.95, PAPERBACK ORIGINAL.

John Sperling, et al., *The Great Divide: Retro vs. Metro America*

Explains how and why our nation is so bitterly divided into what the authors call Retro and Metro America. $19.95, PAPERBACK ORIGINAL.

Curtis White, *The Spirit of Disobedience: Resisting the Charms of Fake Politics, Mindless Consumption, and the Culture of Total Work*

Debunks the notion that liberalism has no need for spirituality and describes a "middle way" through our red state/blue state political impasse. Includes three powerful interviews with John DeGraaf, James Howard Kunstler, and Michael Ableman. $24.00, HARDCOVER.

For more information, please visit www.p3books.com.